Keep It Simple

FOR MOMS ON THE GO

EMILIE BARNES

HARVEST HOUSE™ PUBLISHERS

EUGENE, OREGON

Cover by Terry Dugan Design, Minneapolis, Minnesota

For more information about other books and products
available from Emilie Barnes, please send
a self-addressed, stamped envelope to:

More Hours in My Day
2150 Whitestone Drive
Riverside, CA
92506
(909) 682-4714

Share your favorite hints with us! (Submission
of hints by readers constitutes permission for
accepted hints to be printed in future publications.)

KEEP IT SIMPLE FOR MOMS ON THE GO
Copyright © 2003 by Emilie Barnes
Published by Harvest House Publishers
Eugene, Oregon 97402

Library of Congress Cataloging-in-Publication Data
Barnes, Emilie.
    Keep it simple for moms on the go / Emilie Barnes.
        p. cm.
    ISBN 0-7369-1089-1 (pbk.)
    1. Mothers—Religious life. 2. Christian women—Religious life. I. Title.
    BV4529.18 .B37 2003
    248.8'431—dc21   2002015021

Printed in the United States of America

03   04   05   06   07   08   09   / BP-CF /   10   9   8   7   6   5   4   3   2   1

Contents

January

BEGINNINGS OF CONTENTMENT

Let's Be Practical

> *Paul looked straight at the Sanhedrin and said, "My brothers, I have fulfilled my duty to God in all good conscience to this day."*
>
> ACTS 23:1

Let's be practical about decorating. Being practical really isn't boring. Rather, as you clear away the hassles you will discover that you will have more opportunity to be creative. I have a few questions to ask before you start decorating. They are so simple, yet most people forget to think through some important practical details. These questions will help get you started.

How often are you willing—and able—to clean your house? If you hate dusting, what's the point of all the knickknacks sitting around? Is there anyone allergic to feathers, wool, or other fabrics? What about the needs of small children or pets? Do you have special lighting requirements? Will you be doing a lot of entertaining? You'd be amazed at the number of people who forget to ask the crucial questions and then end up with a beautiful home that *no one* can enjoy—except maybe the decorator! It wouldn't hurt to do a little "inventory" with a friend before you start decorating. It helps to keeps things easy and, of course, simple.

Simple Pleasures

- Plan a personal one-afternoon vacation—choose a destination just a couple of hours away.
- Look at a local college catalog and consider taking a class or seminar.
- Make a goal this week, and then toast its completion with delicious sparkling cider.

Wisdom for Living

*When I see my life through Your eyes, Lord, I know
what matters most. I pray for perspective and discernment
as I make choices about the use of my time.*

Work—A Gift from God

> If they obey and serve him, they will spend the rest of their days in prosperity and their years in contentment.
>
> JOB 36:11

Work doesn't have to be drudgery! It used to be that work was perceived as one of God's blessings. People would do their work "as unto the Lord." Somehow, we seem to have lost that tremendous concept. Many of us today look on work as a penalty or a burden. We struggle to drag ourselves out of bed in the morning to go to that boring job or begin on the drudgery of housework. We live for the weekend instead of appreciating the gift of our daily tasks. I think we'd be a lot happier—and much better workers—if we recaptured the idea that our work, our wealth, and our possessions are all gifts from God.

When we think about how our every action, every deed, every word is a reflection of our relationship with the Lord, it is so important that we put our faith and joy in the work we do, whether that is in the office or the home. We are an example to our children and everyone we make contact with.

As Christians we should be the best workers on our street or in our company. Start your day with a sense of this privileged responsibility, and you'll find that those simple, mundane tasks will become opportunities to honor God. It's pretty simple, don't you think?

Simple Pleasures

* Choose and use words of encouragement today—"good job," "what a blessing," "this is fun."
* Plan for a hard work week and treat yourself to two hours of playtime this weekend.
* Make hot cocoa from scratch and enjoy the aroma and savor the delicious taste.

Wisdom for Living

Father, do You see goodness in the way I handle the tasks assigned to me? I thank You for every chance I have to reflect Your truth. The sacrifice and joy of my work is offered up to You today.

The Blessing of a Smile

When you give it to them, they gather it up; when you open your hand, they are satisfied with good things.

PSALM 104:28

Without words, we can express an enthusiastic hello, affirmation of praise or appreciation, and the joy we are feeling. All with a smile. Do you ever catch yourself smiling when no one is around? Perhaps that is the reason you are smiling. A moment of peace and stillness is a great reason to break into a grin. True joy is hard to hide.

I've never turned down a smile sent in my direction! To me, a smile is a blessing one person can give another. It costs the giver very little, and the receiver takes away a beautiful, unexpected gift. Your smile may be the only smile a person receives today. The Bible says that "wisdom brightens a man's face and changes its hard appearance" (Ecclesiastes 8:1). You've probably heard that it takes more muscles to frown than to smile. True! But a smile still takes a little effort. Noticing another person—and choosing to connect with him or her in order to share something from your heart—takes wisdom. Occasionally, you might find that a smile is not returned, but it's never wasted. Shared blessings never are!

Simple Pleasures

- Buy a mixed bag of hard candy and place it in a glass bowl in the living room.
- Let a piece of butterscotch or peppermint candy remind you that hard work yields sweet success.
- Sip a glass of warm lemon water mid-afternoon for soothing refreshment.

Wisdom for Living

Lord, let me show my joy and Your heart through the gift of a smile. And help me to see the smiles of others as an expression of Your love in my life.

It Doesn't Cost a Fortune

A longing fulfilled is sweet to the soul.

PROVERBS 13:19

Did you know that God has already given you your dream home? Really! It is the one you are in. It is true. Even if you are just starting out, the place you have can be a comfortable—and even beautiful—home!

Get yourself some spray paint and let's get started! Spray white paint on an old wrought-iron lawn table, and you've got yourself a sturdy dining table. Sew some eyelet lace curtains for your windows. I started out in my first apartment with a canvas chair, a box for a lamp table, and an old trunk for a coffee table. I found that if I looked at everyday items with a little different perspective, I found clever uses for them. Ornate family or flea-market silverware arranged in a bright blue terra cotta pot make a functional and never-fading arrangement for the table. Draping scarves over the arms of worn chairs gives them new life and personality. Everywhere you turn, ideas are waiting to be born.

As you dream, and as you plan, build, and decorate, you'll gradually create your dream home. And remember, this is *your* dream home. There are no rules to follow. If a particular color makes you smile, paint a chair, a room, or even a wooden crate in this happy hue. Best of all, as you explore what you like, you are creating a place you can share with friends and family. A place where you can raise your children in the love and admonition of the Lord. Sounds pretty good, doesn't it?

Simple Pleasures

- Remember, you are the management expert for your home.
- When the kids head off to school, light a candle to calmly prepare the rest of your day.
- Walk in the cold morning. It gets you going and clears your mind of yesterday's trouble.

Wisdom for Living

Dear Lord, I dream of a loving, beautiful home that nurtures myself and my family. May You bless the home I am creating today.

9

You Need to Manage Your Money

To the man who pleases him, God gives wisdom, knowledge and happiness.

ECCLESIASTES 2:26

Are you someone who just can't pass up a good deal? When you see something at a discount price, does that item all of a sudden become a need or priority for you? Sometimes a good deal is not nearly as valuable as a good idea! And I happen to have a few of those for you today—free of charge.

You can manage your money better when you have a spiritual purpose for your life. If your spiritual purpose is to serve God, all of your resources minister toward that end. If a good deal has been your budget's downfall, you now have a way to measure the "worth" of that sale item. Ask yourself if it serves your spiritual mission or if it is a choice that provides for the ministry of your family in a necessary way.

Keep in mind that the goal of financial responsibility is financial freedom. To have that kind of freedom, your income needs to exceed your expenses. Your debts need to be paid as they fall due, and—above all—you need to be content with your present income level. Make regular giving a family priority. And recognize that God owns everything. Your home, your car, your marriage, your children, your job—everything. You may possess them, but you don't own them. God says: "The silver is mine and the gold is mine" (Haggai 2:8).

Simple Pleasures

- Seek God's Word today for a deeper understanding of your spiritual purpose.
- List three ways you want to use your money this year to serve God.
- Think of a special treat you can buy for yourself this year. Set a goal and work toward it.

Wisdom for Living

Lord, I want to be rich, rich, rich...in spirit! I want my money to serve a spiritual purpose. Let my heart and purse be discerning when the "bargains" of the world appear.

Mary, Martha, and Me

> His master replied, "Well done, good and faithful servant! You have been faithful with a few things; I will put you in charge of many things. Come and share your master's happiness!"
>
> MATTHEW 25:21

I have to admit to you that I am often more like Martha than Mary. I become so focused on perfection that I lose sight of God's perfect ways. Jesus said of one sister: "Mary has chosen what is better, and it will not be taken away from her" (Luke 10:42).

It's a dilemma, isn't it? We desire to be like Mary—but Martha is always getting in the way. My Martha side wants my home to be clean and in order for my guests. I'm sure Martha mopped, dusted, and cleaned all day. My Mary side says housework can wait; Jesus is more important. I can tidy up after He goes on His way. I need a balance in my tidiness and my passion for other people's needs. Both have to be addressed. We must learn to say no to good things so that we can save our yes for the very best.

Do you have moments in your schedule this week where you can apply this principle? Try being Mary this time. Take mental notes, or even journal the experience. See how God will change your heart and your perspective regarding an event or activity. I'd be curious whether your children or husband will notice the change when your Mary side makes an appearance in your home.

Simple Pleasures

- Choose a new perfume or color of lipstick for this year.
- Do five minutes of stretching before your devotion time and feel yourself relax.
- Paint your fingernails a fun color to make up for a darker part of the year.

Wisdom for Living

I so like control, Lord. I give this over to You.
May I recognize the very best things You set before me in each
circumstance. I don't want to miss any one of them!

Free to Be Godly Women

*I know what it is to be in need, and
I know what it is to have plenty. I
have learned the secret of being
content in any and every situation,
whether well fed or hungry,
whether living in plenty or in want.*

PHILIPPIANS 4:12

You don't have to prove yourself to anyone. Whew! Isn't that good to hear? But sometimes that is hard to believe. Keep your focus on being a godly woman. Let's look at how that perspective gives you real freedom.

To me, a godly woman doesn't have to prove herself to anyone. She's strong, yet she doesn't use her strength to control people. She doesn't depend on recognition from others. She has a deep awareness of God's love for her. That kind of peace, strength, and confidence comes from depending on God, drawing on His strength, and learning to be like Him. When that happens we're free of being competitive. There's no need to prove our value. We know how much we are worth in God's sight. It's then we're transformed into the lovely women God created us to be. It's then we're free to reach out in love to others.

When you seek His will and tap into His strength, you will experience the freedom to enjoy who you are. It is permission to be the special mom your children have been blessed with. Knowing your value is secured in heaven is such a gift. Embrace it today.

Simple Pleasures

- Give one thing to God this morning and then don't worry about it again.
- Cook pancakes for your kids. Use chocolate chips to make a smiley face on each one.
- Wear two different socks or shoes this morning and then give a treat to the child who notices first.

Wisdom for Living

*I use so much energy seeking the approval of others, Lord.
Let me rejoice in who You made me to be.
And let me embrace the godly woman I can become.*

Don't Plan to Fail

> Then I realized that it is good and proper for a man to eat and drink, and to find satisfaction in his toilsome labor under the sun during the few days of life God has given him—for this is his lot.
>
> ECCLESIASTES 5:18

Are you familiar with the saying "successful people do what unsuccessful people aren't willing to do"? We all have 24 hours or 1440 minutes or 86,400 seconds in a day. To get the most out of life, we all have to make wise decisions based on what life means to each of us. We don't plan to fail, but we'll fail every time if we don't plan to succeed. Success doesn't come by luck or accident—it comes because we schedule a plan and plan a schedule.

When it comes to money, you must have a plan or you won't be able to make good daily decisions. When it comes to organizing your day, you need to know what priorities are at the top of the list. When it comes to decisions for the family, you need to be following the plan you and your spouse have for your life. When it comes to ministry, you need to be aware of the gifts God has given you so you can focus on areas of ministry He will place before you.

Remember, no plans for the future muddy the water in deciding what to do today.

Simple Pleasures

- Interview someone in your life whom you view as a success. Learn from them.
- Read the book of Proverbs and take in some valuable teachings for a successful life.
- Tear out a picture from a magazine that reminds you of a goal you have set. Put it on your bathroom mirror or the refrigerator.

Wisdom for Living

I want to live a life of purpose—Your purpose, Lord.
Please show me the way.

We Need to Give

*Let no debt remain outstanding,
except the continuing debt to love
one another, for he who loves his
fellowman has fulfilled the law.*

ROMANS 13:8

Once I heard a comedian say, "I've been rich and I've been poor—and I like being rich better!" For the Christian, the only reason to be rich is to have resources to carry on God's program. God certainly doesn't need our wealth, and He doesn't need our possessions. But *we* need to give. When we lovingly and obediently fulfill our role as givers—no matter what the amount—God will use those offerings to minister to others.

It's interesting how many people don't plan their giving in the budget. It should be our firstfruits. The money needs to be set aside as it's earned and then given systematically. It's part of keeping life simple, isn't it? God is always first!

Don't get caught up in thinking "when we have this or make this much we will start giving" because it won't happen. You are creating your habits for giving now...every day. Everything you have belongs to God. Giving back to Him should happen no matter what your income or circumstances. And the ultimate result is that you will be blessed.

Look at how you give of yourself, your time, your money. Does it glorify the One who has given you many blessings?

Simple Pleasures

* Think of your past sins as a great debt. Now think of Jesus settling each and every one.
* Forgive someone's debt to you. Give them some freedom. You will feel lighter too.
* Write out a budget for your time. It is so much fun to choose time to give to charity.

Wisdom for Living

Lord, I want to develop a way of life that is focused on giving back to You. Let me be wise and in balance as I provide and care for my family and reach out to others. I seek You in every decision.

The Big Thing

Now that you have purified yourselves by obeying the truth so that you have sincere love for your brothers, love one another deeply, from the heart.

1 PETER 1:22

Let's talk about that "Big Thing" in your living room. It may be a piano, a sideboard, or a beautiful armoire. Make it the focal point of attention. If it's a piano, why not emphasize your musical interest? Frame an old piece of sheet music and hang it on the wall—or decorate the wall with old banjos or violins. Paint an old magazine rack or decoupage it with sheet music and tuck it beside the piano bench to hold music.

If the large item is an heirloom piece, for example, a buffet or vintage chair, gather and frame photos of the people who have at one time or another owned and used the piece. How grand it would be to be seated among the images of your ancestors, knowing that their lives are connected to yours in so many ways.

Sometimes that large focal point is a window. Maximize it with elegant drapes or colored blinds. Set it off as a piece of art so that it can be appreciated from every angle in the room. Place furniture so that those seated can benefit from the view and from the light coming through the window. See how easy this can be.

Someone once said, "The best homes seem to come from the heart and are created by people who know who they are and express it." Go ahead, express yourself.

Simple Pleasures

- Get rid of a big eyesore by moving it to storage or giving it away.
- Drape several yards of fabric over a curtain rod to add new contrast to your curtains.
- Hang a small stained glass piece in the kitchen to add color to your view from the sink.

Wisdom for Living

Help me to seek You as my focal point all through the day, Lord. May Your love be larger than life in my home.

Fabric Tricks

Keep your lives free from the love of money and be content with what you have, because God has said, "Never will I leave you; never will I forsake you."

HEBREWS 13:5

Today I want you to consider the freedom of fabric! Decorating with fabric can provide so many ways to change the look of a room or your entire home. You will wonder why you haven't focused on it before.

If you're concerned about mixing fabrics and colors—don't be! Go ahead. You can successfully mix as many as ten patterns if you keep a common color as a thread. Tiny stripes, large and small prints, plaids, and novelty designs. You name it—just tie them all together with a common color. You might feel as though you are breaking a rule, but just wait and see how the room will turn out. Beautiful!

For a very small space or a room filled with mismatched furniture, use one fabric throughout for slipcovers, pillows, and window coverings. The look will be quite sophisticated and soothing. Whenever you see a length of cute, inexpensive fabric on a sale table, snatch it up! You can find so many lovely patterns now in sheet fabric that you will start to see sheets as future curtains, duvets, and wall treatments.

Fabric is a wonderful way to infuse your home with texture, pattern, and color. Let it remind you of the many different people God brings into your life and into your home. Be thankful for the richness they add to your own style.

Simple Pleasures

- Add a blanket or quilt to a sofa or chair for new texture.
- Take up knitting or crocheting and make small, colorful coasters for your end tables.
- Create an indoor flower box to add cheer to any window this winter.

Wisdom for Living

Lord, I know the intricate detail of my life's pattern is part of the fabric of faith and Your love. May I provide warmth and inspiration to my family today and every day.

The Gift of Hospitality

And I—in righteousness I will see your face; when I awake, I will be satisfied with seeing your likeness.

PSALM 17:15

As the Lord prepares a place in His house for you, think of how you can share His love with others as you prepare a guest room. What extra touches will soothe a traveling friend, comfort a healing visitor, or welcome an unexpected guest?

Some creative touches can make a big statement—simple things that say "I care." Make sure your guest room has a well-placed reading lamp. Add some books and magazines and a cozy chair. Look for some comfortable, inexpensive slippers to have on hand for visitors; be sure to have pairs that suit both men and women. A good clock radio provides both music and a sense of independence—and don't forget fruit and a pitcher of water for midnight munchies. Before bed prepare your guest a cup of chamomile tea and serve it with lemon cookies or ginger snaps.

Flowers, lovely pictures, and scented candles (check for allergies!) all create a welcoming touch. I love to bring my guests a morning tray. It's become our trademark. Along with coffee or tea and toast and jelly, I add a card with a morning Scripture verse or provide them with a daily devotional already marked for the new day.

All it takes is a little imagination, a little creativity—and your guests will feel right at home!

Simple Pleasures

* Look around your house. What reminds you of God in each room?
* For out-of-town guests, serve specialty pastries from a local bakery.
* Have lots of fruit on hand for you, children, and guests to enjoy often.

Wisdom for Living

I cannot wait to see the room You are preparing for me, Lord.
I imagine the warmth and security and peace I will feel,
and I pray that I can offer this comfort in my home.

Bright Ideas

You may have collections you didn't know you had! And you can turn them into decorating gold! Aren't you excited to know this? First, check out those hand-me-down treasures from a favorite relative—an old hymnbook, a church fan, a Scripture bookmark, a childhood photo. Pictures with a related theme are always interesting. Travel mementos, old books, dishes with similar designs, even costume jewelry.

If you do not have hand-me-down treasures, go and get some for yourself. Visit estate sales and antique sales and wisely select a few inexpensive items to start a collection of vintage pieces. Maybe you prefer old books or glassware. Maybe linens and dolls fit your personality and will also be treasures that will be fun to pass along to your daughter some day.

Chances are, there are items you didn't even know you had. And when they are paired with like-colored or themed items, they have a whole new life ahead of them. And you have a new look for a room.

Take a look around. You probably have some decorating "gold" just waiting to be mined!

Simple Pleasures

- Remind yourself of some of your best ideas in the past five years.
- Start a collection of poetry in a journal or a scrapbook.
- Write down a New Year's list of hopes you have for your children.

Wisdom for Living

I cannot hide from You, Lord. You know everything about me just as You have known everything about my ancestors. Let my life follow a faithful heritage. Let me share Your gift of salvation with generations to come.

Being an Example

If we have food and clothing, we will be content with that.

1 TIMOTHY 6:8

Are our actions consistent with what we say we believe? That is a tough one no matter whom you are. But it is especially important when you are a mom. Have you ever had your unkind words or expressions come back to you in a miniature reenactment through your child? Oh, what a sinking feeling. But being consistent in behavior, attitude, and discipline is not just important because you have children. It is important because you are a child of God.

Little eyes are often watching how we behave when no one is looking. We may talk calmness and patience, but how do we respond when we're standing in a long line at the market? How does our conversation go when there's a slowdown on the highway? Do we help people even when it's not convenient? We are continually setting some kind of example whether we know it or not. Be a good neighbor today. Mail a thank-you card to someone who's done something for you. Call a friend, send an e-mail. Let your life be a simple example to all those around you.

And when your children get older and you are standing in the store alone, growing impatient in the ten-item line, remember that God is always watching. Do not disappoint Him. Make Him proud of His child today.

Simple Pleasures

- Thank God for being an attentive parent every day.
- Thank your children for being great people.
- If you feel impatient, think of five blessings before you say anything.

Wisdom for Living

Lord, I need Your guidance to be a role model for my children.
Help me to always be an example of a godly woman.
Let them never doubt my integrity.

Your Stylish Self

Put on the new self, created to be like God in true righteousness and holiness.

EPHESIANS 4:24

What's your decorating style? Before you answer, remember style is not *what* you have, it's what you *do* with what you have. Decorating with style is merely taking your tastes, your personality, and your possessions and showing their best face to the world. What you love, what activities you enjoy, how you work…these are all issues of style. As a mom, you might feel that you have lost a bit of yourself in the process. Don't let that happen. You do have a style that is all your own. Sure, your life might be filled with cartoon characters and crayon drawings and sippy cups, but you are still you. And staying true to that self is important. God made you. Don't unmake you.

My advice? Take a little journey of self-discovery. Shop in all the places you can't afford. I said *shop*—not *buy!* Notice the woods, the fabrics, the color schemes. Look through magazines and clip out what you like. In fact, pour yourself a cup of tea, take your magazines, and let 'er rip! It won't be long before you'll begin to see a picture of what your style really is. And that's the best place to start.

Simple Pleasures

- Add a red scarf to your seasonal accessories.
- Go through your closet and toss anything that is not your style.
- Do the same in each room of your house.

Wisdom for Living

Help me rediscover what I love most about life, Lord. These bits and pieces of me make me whole, and they help me share myself with my family. I want to be who You made me to be!

Family Strength

I have fellowship offerings at home; today I fulfilled my vows.

PROVERBS 7:14

My husband Bob and I have enjoyed years of marriage, raised two children, and welcomed sweet grandchildren. In my ministry I've had the opportunity to talk to thousands of women, and there are certain characteristics that seem to account for much of the success, happiness, and strength of families in America.

Characteristics like an awareness that each member is appreciated. A voluntary desire to spend time together that is great in both quantity and quality. Create times of togetherness when your children are little so that it is always natural for your family to sit and talk or read from Scripture together. These traditions help build strong ties that hold fast when communication is at a low point. Which leads to another important characteristic—good communication. Open communication. Let us not forget a high degree of religious orientation. Also a strong commitment to make the family succeed. And the ability to deal with a crisis in a positive manner.

If by the power of God we could wake up each morning to the idea we were going to be a blessing to members of our family, no matter what, can you imagine the impact we would have? Go a step further, and think about how you can be a blessing to everyone you interact with this day. Wow! What a difference *you* can make. Pretty simple—yet pretty profound!

Simple Pleasures

- Pray with your husband about your family's success and happiness.
- Create a basic mission statement for your family.
- Plan an evening with the children to share the mission statement and to pray about it.

Wisdom for Living

God, bless us with a strong family. May we seek Your Word and guidance as we build the foundation this family needs. May I be a blessing to my husband and to my children.

Your Material Assets

He waters the mountains from his upper chambers; the earth is satisfied by the fruit of his work.

PSALM 104:13

How are your "material" assets? No, don't go check your savings account...I mean real material. Do you use fabric to add beauty to your home? If yes, let's look at what you have done and think of new projects. If no, then are you in store for some fun!

You don't have to be a professional seamstress. Forget the sewing and grab the glue gun! Fabrics can easily add charm and texture to your room. Slipcovers are like a magic wand. A simple straight chair draped with tulle and tied with a satin ribbon is a wonderful touch for a bedroom. Or transform that folding chair by slipping a pillowcase over the back and tying the base with ribbon. You're laughing—but you try it! That is all I ask. Start with one room, focus on one corner or one piece of furniture that could really use some renewal, and go for it.

Fabric is a great revitalizer in your home. Speaking of revitalizers! When was the last time you grabbed a cold glass of tea, picked out a comfortable spot—Bible and notebook in hand—and spent some time revitalizing your heart? Our hearts can become worn and faded. Dress your heart in the texture and beauty of God's Word. You have never looked so good! Go ahead, treat yourself. Today is the perfect day for it.

Simple Pleasures

* If you reupholster a family heirloom, place a bit of the old fabric in a shadow box.
* With your children or a friend, make fabric book covers to protect old favorites.
* Use sheets to create curtains for a child's room or the kitchen.

Wisdom for Living

Revitalize me, Lord. Oh, how my soul is thirsty and tired.
Your Word fills me and clothes me with royal fabric.
I am dressed by the Prince of Peace!

Now Would Be Good

The fear of the LORD leads to life:
Then one rests content, untouched
by trouble.

PROVERBS 19:23

I want God to work everything out...*now!* Don't you sometimes feel this way too? Maybe your child is having trouble at home or school. Maybe you are worried about an upcoming commitment you made. Maybe you are scared about your circumstances.

I can offer you what works for me when I grow impatient about life. I read God's Word. Psalm 69:17-18 says: "Don't hide from me, for I am in deep trouble. Quick! Come and save me. Come, Lord and rescue me" (TLB). The truth of the matter is that God *will* rescue me, but in His time and not at my hurried pace. In fact, while I am fretting about not receiving help, maybe help is already on the way or within reach. I just have to trust His timing and commitment to me, His child. He hears my cries. And I certainly appreciate God's loving patience with me in the midst of the process.

Let's pray together. "Father God, slow me down. You are great and awesome. Thank You for the simple reminders of who You are and what You have done. Put a strong desire in my soul to spend time with You today in prayer and study. Let time stand still and let me forget all about my schedule. Amen."

Simple Pleasures

- Set the kitchen timer for five minutes. Spend the time in absolute quiet and stillness.
- Ask God for help. Be specific.
- Use each red light you encounter to praise God for one thing.

Wisdom for Living

I wait upon Your Word for my life, Lord.
Gladly I wait for Your good and perfect will.

Know What You Want

A mess in the home can sometimes mean a messy life. I know I might be treading on some sensitive toes. I don't mean that a woman who puts her family ahead of perfectionism on the cleaning front is wrong. In fact, that can be a good priority system. But I do think that when your home is out of control, it *might* represent more than just your style of housekeeping. Are you feeling stressed? Overwhelmed? Pulled in at least 20 directions? Goals are a solution.

Taking the time to set goals is basic. Goals help us clean out the messes that prevent us from doing the things we want to do but don't have time to do. Ask: Where are you going? What do you need to get there? Does this save you money? Does this save you time? Does this improve the quality of your life? These are excellent questions to ask before you do almost any activity, but especially one that is time consuming or one that just seems exhausting every time you think about it.

We need to be careful not to choose a lifestyle that promotes "discontentment." A messy life and clutter in our personal affairs can be awfully frustrating. You'll be amazed at how understanding this concept will change your life! It's very simple! The pursuits and goals we choose will help us grow into the women God wants us to become.

Simple Pleasures

You will succeed best when you put the restless anxious side of affairs out of mind, and allow the restful side to live in your thoughts.

—MARGARET STOWE

Wisdom for Living

I choose to be content, Lord. I see the blessings that surround me, and I am grateful. I see what needs to be done because I have focused on goals that are pleasing to You.

Handmade

*Give her of the fruit of her hands,
and let her own works praise her in
the gates.*

PROVERBS 31:31 NKJV

Handmade! The very word says "treasure" to me. Today we don't *need* to weave or sew. Making something by hand is entirely optional. We don't *need* to quilt or knit or whittle or hammer. Choosing to make something by hand often means a sacrifice of leisure time. You're making a deliberate investment of yourself for the sake of someone you care about. Think how much more value that adds to the gift or to the treasure you want to have in your home.

Working with your hands can be deeply satisfying. It's such a joy to produce something useful, something beautiful, something that memories are attached to. You may not be a professional artist, but neither were most of the people whose handiwork we cherish today. Make it a family activity. Encourage your children to learn a skill or craft like crocheting, woodworking, carving, or painting. Their lives will be richer as they come to appreciate craftsmanship and hard work.

When was the last time you explored a craft? You might have something partially completed in a dresser drawer. Spend time enjoying creative inspiration and expression. Bring back the importance of hand-made treasures to your daily life.

Simple Pleasures

- Go to a fabric store for a brainstorming session. Take in the rich colors and textures.
- Host a painting party for your children. Use watercolors and enjoy a colorful afternoon.
- Spend 15 minutes rearranging wall hangings in one room. Try to find a fresh look.

Wisdom for Living

*Lord, Your wonders are all around me. I marvel at Your creativity.
I am a handmade treasure. My worth is in the care
and love You poured into my life.*

Little Eyes

To the faithful you show yourself faithful, to the blameless you show yourself blameless.

PSALM 18:25

You are probably aware that your children are watching to see how you behave when no one's looking. Talk with calmness and patience, show God's love, be gentle with others and accepting of people. Here are a few tips that have helped me: We can be good neighbors. We can send thank-you notes after receiving a gift. We can show our appreciation for kindness sent our way. We can pick up after ourselves after a picnic or even at a fast-food restaurant. We're continually setting some kind of example whether we know it or not...or whether we like it or not.

Sometimes it is an example for someone else. Perhaps a neighbor who is not a Christian will see the difference. The stranger who receives your generosity or encouragement will see the difference. And as you "do unto others," your child will see a living example of Christlike behavior. And when they come to a place of believing in the Lord, they will understand what that means for a life. How actions and words do reflect God in our everyday interactions.

Do we have to be perfect? No, not at all. But we do need to set an example. We are so lucky to have the Lord as an example and an encouragement. Be one of His faithful servants in the eyes of your children.

Simple Pleasures

- Encourage your child with words from Scripture today.
- Build up a stranger in some way as you go about your business this week.
- When you have a negative thought about someone, immediately think of something good about them as well. Soon, those positive responses will come more naturally.

Wisdom for Living

I will honor You, Lord, with my actions and my words.
May all that I do direct my children to the ways of God.

February

DISCOVERING YOUR HEART

Where Is Your Treasure?

For where your treasure is, there your heart will be also.

MATTHEW 6:21

Jesus said long ago that our hearts will be found in the vicinity of our treasures. Our timeless treasures symbolize our values, don't they? Love, joy, beauty, hope, family. A delicate cut-glass vase, a set of antique tools, a child's drawing, a grandfather's watch. All timeless treasures—because they bring to mind our most loved relationships. Our dearest memories.

Where are your treasures right now? Dig into storage boxes, flip through old photos, look at your grandmother's old Bible. Pick up these items one by one and share them with your children. Dust off that old scrapbook and turn those old hankies you collected into that baby quilt you wanted to make. When special belongings are incorporated into your daily surroundings, you will be encouraged by their presence and the people or places they bring to mind.

Your timeless treasures represent your heritage, your love, and your memories. Often these heirlooms also share a testimony of faith, perseverance, and trust in the Lord. Displaying these pieces of your past and your family's journey is a simple way to share the greatest story of all time—the one of Jesus' love.

Simple Pleasures

- Make cutout hearts with your children. Write down one life treasure on each.
- Have a dish of those cinnamon heart-shaped candies handy for an afternoon treat.
- Do something good for your heart. Sign up for a charity walk or organize one!

Wisdom for Living

*Lord, let the treasures of my past remind me of Your love
and of the treasure of heaven, which awaits me in my future.*

A House Where Love Lives

Speak to one another with psalms, hymns and spiritual songs. Sing and make music in your heart to the Lord.

I have some ideas for a "warmhearted" welcome to your home. Even though I have not had the pleasure of seeing where you live, I can help you tap into your home's love appeal.

What part of your home do you enjoy most? Is it the view? The yard? Let that be the focus of your entertaining and your hospitality. Have fun sharing the aspects of your life that bring you the most pleasure. For instance, one of the big hits in our guest bathroom is a big, fluffy terry robe hanging on the back of the bathroom door. Other extras we offer our guests include a travel iron and small ironing board, books and toys for visiting children, a blow-dryer, notepaper and pen, literature on local attractions, and disposable cameras.

Hospitality can be extended even if your guests stay in a hotel. Have a floral arrangement sent to their room. Leave a basket of homemade muffins at the desk for when they arrive. If your guests have children, leave a gift certificate for the local ice cream shop. Let them know they're welcome!

Remembering the little blessings that make you happy will help you do the same for others. What simple joys did God give you today? Pass them on!

Simple Pleasures

- Bring a coworker a latte to help start her day off with a smile.
- Take some of your shoes and clothes to a women's shelter.
- Volunteer to chaperone your child's school field trips.

Wisdom for Living

Lord, I know the comforts of home are for sharing.
Please give me a sensitivity to the needs my guests have. Don't let me
forget to also show them Your comfort for their spiritual needs.

29

Tea Party Fun

Love the LORD your God with all your heart and with all your soul and with all your strength.

DEUTERONOMY 6:5

Tea parties are not just for a gathering of girlfriends. The comfort of fellowship served with tea can minister to everyone. Male, female, young, old. Come one, come all.

I invite you to try out a few of these ideas. See how the simple act of providing tea turns into the fulfillment of God's commandment to "love thy neighbor..."

Try sending a birthday tea party—in a box! Once I received one with everything I needed to celebrate: a wonderful Mississippi mud cake, napkins, tablecloth, box of teabags, artificial flowers, and a book of poems. What a great spirit lifter! Or share midnight tea with a loved one. After a busy day, Bob and I often sit down and unwind over a cup of herbal tea. Or host an "adopt a grandma" or "adopt a kid" tea. Have everyone bring a guest who is over sixty or under eight. It's also great for teenagers. The idea is to spend time with new friends or old friends. It can be a wonderful time of sharing what God has done in your lives.

If you work with a youth group or Sunday school class, teas are a wonderful way for your church family to become closer.

Simple Pleasures

- Buy or borrow a book on tea. Become acquainted with the wonders of this timeless tradition.
- Invite one of the women from church over for tea. Enjoy a new, deeper friendship.
- Make some delicious cinnamon scones and share them with your children after school.

Wisdom for Living

Father, whom can I host today? What will I learn
about You when I invite new friends into my circle of life?
I want to love You with all my heart.

A friend loves at all times.

As women we must be in touch with the needs of our friends. That is true friendship. It is not always easy to keep up with people and their needs when our own feel so consuming. When you have those feelings, those moments when you sense you should call an old friend or check in on someone—do it! If you have ever been on the receiving end of someone being faithful to this tug on their heartstrings, you know how good it feels to sense God is taking care of you through your friends.

I can't encourage you enough to stay in tune with those you hold close to your heart. Simply listen as they talk and pray as you listen. I have a friend's photo on the door of our refrigerator. Each time I open that door, I pray for her. It could be 20 times a day. Although we're busy women, we can devote our hearts to prayer as we come and go in our daily business.

My prayer today is, "Father God, help me to be reminded to bring before You those who hurt, who are ill, and who are spiritually weak. Bring to my mind today that friend who needs a special touch from You, our heavenly Father. Thank You."

Simple Pleasures

- Prepare postcards with addresses and stamps for quick notes to friends near or far.
- Look at your birthday calendar. Pray for every friend celebrating a birthday this month.
- Introduce yourself to someone new this week at church, work, and the neighborhood.

Wisdom for Living

Lord, help me to hear Your voice speaking to my heart.
When You remind me to pray for a friend or call a family member,
I want to be quick to respond to that holy nudge.
Thank You for the wonderful people You put in my life.

Home Is in the Kitchen

But if from there you seek the LORD your God, you will find him if you look for him with all your heart and with all your soul.

DEUTERONOMY 4:29

"No matter where I serve my guests—it seems they like my kitchen best!"

That little saying is so much more than just a cute rhyme. It's the way I feel. The kitchen is the place in my home where warmth and love reign. What memories!

Make your kitchen a room you enjoy! How do you feel about it right now? Does it feel like a place of chaos or work? Or does it feed your spirit each time you are there? Find ways to make the kitchen a nourishing room for you and your family. Hang pots on hooks above the stove, line the kitchen window ledge with plants, and don't forget pictures! Arrange a "love wall" at one end of the kitchen and fill it with great picture memories. The point is, in these hectic days you want a place where your family feels at home simply and lovingly.

Don't forget to make room for conversation in the kitchen. Encourage your children to come and talk with you or do their homework while you are cooking dinner. Have a comfy chair in the corner with a small table if you have room. This will be an invitation to enjoy the heart of your home.

Simple Pleasures

- Create meals for the week on Saturday so you can spend evenings with your family.
- Create baking mixes in advance so that cakes and other goodies can be made quickly.
- Make a double batch of your favorite cookie dough. Freeze a portion for treats later.

Wisdom for Living

Father, I want a cozy kitchen so that my family is nourished physically and spiritually. I want it to be a place of thanksgiving for the blessings of Your abundant provision.

It's a Frame Up

But be sure to fear the LORD and serve him faithfully with all your heart; consider what great things he has done for you.

1 SAMUEL 12:24

Frames! They're the latest decorating accessory. You see them everywhere in all kinds of shapes and sizes. I thought it might be fun to share some ideas for what to frame and what to hang.

How about interesting old letters or postcards? Children's artwork or old report cards? Seashells from the beach? Magazine covers? The possibilities are unlimited—just use your imagination. I love to see a beautiful afghan or quilt hanging on a wall. Clocks, trays, tiles, and musical instruments all look wonderful in just the right wall setting. Make your home a place that reflects who you are. One friend of mine has Bible verses beautifully displayed in different ways throughout her home. It says so much about her and is such a simple way to reach out to others.

What can your framed objects share about you? Maybe your passion for gardening or your love for old family photos. Create a "picture" of who you are and place it within a beautiful frame.

Simple Pleasures

- Are you lucky enough to have handwritten letters from a grandparent? Frame them!
- Let your child write out a Scripture for the week and hang it by the front door.
- Plan for a family portrait to be taken. You will be so glad to have this treasure.

Wisdom for Living

Lord, sharing my life with others includes sharing my favorite pastimes or treasures throughout my home. May each special touch reflect a picture of You.

A Dream with a Deadline

For wisdom will enter your heart, and knowledge will be pleasant to your soul.

PROVERBS 2:10

A goal is nothing more than a "dream with a deadline." Isn't that a great way to think of them? Dreams are wonderful. So are goals. Making them happen is tremendous!

Proverbs 29:18 says if we have no vision, we perish (KJV). You're either moving ahead or falling back—there's no middle ground. Remember that goal-setting must include: 1) how much and 2) a deadline to complete. For example: "I would like to lose 15 pounds by June 15." And cut yourself some slack. Goals aren't cast in concrete. They just point you in the right direction.

You might want to make a list of the areas of your life where goals are important. Physical...relational...financial...professional...spiritual. You get the idea! Start setting goals and be sure to make them measurable!

You can make this a family activity as well. Around the dinner table ask each person what their goal is for the next week, month, or even year. Your children will see how important dreams are and how a family can help one another reach their goals. After the discussion, pray for each person's goal.

Simple Pleasures

- Read one of your old journals to see how your goals have been reached or changed.
- Start a journal if you do not have one. Record those dreams with deadlines!
- Encourage the dreams of your child. Celebrate their talents and goals.

Wisdom for Living

Through faith, a dream of eternal life is granted.
I ask that You would fill my life with goals that are pleasing to You,
Lord. May they carry out Your dreams for me and my family.

Fill Your Home

I praise you because I am fearfully and wonderfully made; your works are wonderful, I know that full well.

PSALM 139:14

Fill your home with things that remind you of who you are—and what you love. There is nobody else like you. Celebrate this wonderful truth. God does!

I feel immediately at home in houses where people have surrounded themselves with what they love. It also gives us something to talk about. Don't you feel welcome and comfortable in a room that reflects the owner's personality? And have you ever noticed that even if there is a variety of elements or styles within a home like this, they all seem to go together? God is good!

I feel the same way in my own rooms because there's so much of me in them. Clusters of family photos, a teacup collection, books and signs and plaques collected on trips. A verse of Scripture. Somehow it all comes together to say, "This is who we are. This is what we love." The point of it all is making yourself and other people feel at home.

Trust yourself. Let your home reflect the wonder and beauty that God created in you and in each member of your family. You cannot go wrong!

Simple Pleasures

* Does your home still reflect the person who lived there before you moved there? Start brainstorming!
* Include touches of comfort from your childhood. Your children will find comfort in them too.
* Place books on gardening, decorating, or landscaping on the coffee table for enjoyable moments of planning.

Wisdom for Living

I want to celebrate the me You made, Lord. Help me discover my personal style and the inspiration I can offer my own home.

First Impressions Count

Yet if you devote your heart to him and stretch out your hands to him...then you will lift up your face without shame; you will stand firm and without fear.

Your mother was right—first impressions *do* count! With a little thought and a little caring, your home can be inviting. Let's consider this, though. Before someone even enters, what does your home say to them? What impression are you making? Let's create the sense of a warm smile and a loving heart.

But where to begin? How about at the curb? A whimsical mailbox by the driveway, for instance, says a happy hello to anyone who approaches. A curving walkway dotted with lamps and flowers directs your guests to your door. And a good, old-fashioned welcome mat offers a gracious invitation to enter.

More importantly, you begin with a hospitable heart, a willingness to share your life, and a desire to make space in your plans for friends, family, and strangers. From there, it's just a little planning and a little creativity—and you're all set. Devote your home to sharing the heart of God.

It won't be long and your house will have the unmistakable message: "You're welcome here! We're thrilled to see you! Come in and make yourself at home!"

Simple Pleasures

* Decorate your mailbox for the season.
* Plant flowers at varying heights so some are at a child's eye level.
* Place an arrangement of silk flowers on a windowsill for wintertime color.

Wisdom for Living

Heavenly Father, let my home shout "Welcome to my life, my family, and my Lord!" May the first impression people receive from me always be one of kindness and an invitation to friendship.

A Sense of Love

Know therefore that the LORD your God is God; he is the faithful God, keeping his covenant of love to a thousand generations of those who love him and keep his commands.

DEUTERONOMY 7:9

How are you at developing a sense of love in your family? Do they "feel the love"? There are so many simple ways for you to build a foundation of expressed love. Don't let another day go by without trying one of these ideas or maybe other thoughts you have that you just have not gotten around to. Never delay saying "I love you."

Buy a packet of assorted colored cards and have them preprinted to say, "I love you because..." Use them to write a personal message to a child: "Dear Katy, I love you because you always come to the breakfast table with a smile. Love, Mom." What a great way to start the day. Put a card under a pillow, by a toothbrush, in a sack lunch, or even mail it to your child in a special envelope. Come to think about it, your spouse might like to find one too!

Nurture a generation of children who love the Lord. When a child does something that makes you smile, tell them right away. Maybe you caught them sharing or caring for one of their friends. Maybe they encouraged you with a hug or an encouraging word. This reinforces positive behavior, and it lets every family member know they are special.

Simple Pleasures

- Say prayers of thanksgiving before your meals. Thank God out loud for your children.
- Start a promise journal where your family can record how God is faithful over the years.
- Plan a date with each of your children. Start the date with a prayer and a hug.

Wisdom for Living

Saying "I love you" is one of the easiest and most important things I can do as a mother. Help me, Lord, to never miss an opportunity to shower my family with love.

Get the Picture?

I will perpetuate your memory through all generations; therefore the nations will praise you for ever and ever.

PSALM 45:17

When you get creative with your home décor, often it is the cheap idea that shouts "clever, charming, and personal." You do not have to spend much at all to create a room that reflects your personality and your family's style.

A wall of photographs is a great expression of what you love. For a museum look, use black and white photos with wide white mats and thin black frames. Pictures don't always have to be framed. Try mounting an inexpensive print on a tray or a piece of board. Cover the edges with ribbon or fabric trim.

Stop spending money and start spending time looking at your wall as a large, blank canvas. Soon you will get a feeling for how to create a picture on that canvas. A combination of images and objects, lines and textures, reflects who you are.

See, it doesn't take money when you give more of yourself to the project. In all that you do, praise the Lord for your many blessings and let the work of your hands be a sacrifice for Him. Honor Him with the home you are making today.

Simple Pleasures

- Make a collage using color copies of favorite family photos. Get the kids involved!
- Place children's school photos along a ribbon and loop along the hallway like cake icing.
- Spend a morning sifting through boxes of photos. Just enjoy the memories!

Wisdom for Living

Lord, let me always be mindful that within the framework of faith, I am creating a work of art. I am creating a home filled with a loving family.

A Few Hat Tricks

Wondering where to hang your hat? Place these ideas at the top of your décor list and take pleasure in the sense of flair that hats offer. Take that antique bonnet from great-grandma's attic and group it with a little purse and an antique photo. Or line up several hats over a window. Stack straw hats in a corner or on a table. I have a friend who loves to wear hats. When they're not in use, she displays them on decorative hooks in her bedroom. You could take a hat and decorate it with silk flowers as a gift arrangement for a friend. Turn a straw hat upside down, lace ribbon across the top to use as a handle and you have a romantic basket perfect for gift giving and for displaying items in the home.

For your children, decorate their rooms with hats they might like— baseball caps, childhood bonnets, Mickey Mouse ears from last year's vacation. Let them have fun with it.

The whole idea is to make the place where you live a creative expression of who you are! If hats aren't your thing, choose whatever is "tops" to you and have fun!

Simple Pleasures

Once you see, you appreciate and then you become inspired.

—ALEXANDRIA STODDARD

Wisdom for Living

Lord, I rejoice in Your spirit of creativity and inspiration. You make my life beautiful. You decorate my heart with Your love, mercy, and hope. Thank You, Lord.

Table Art

No matter how much cupboard or closet space you have, it is still nice to have deliberately arranged objects on the top of tables, dressers, mantles, and windowsills. Decide which pieces you own that you would like to showcase.

To add interest to dresser tops (or any flat surface in your home), create a "tablescape." It's simply artfully arranged still life featuring items you love. For your husband's dresser, it could be a painted tray for pocket items or a group of photos in silver frames. Yours could be a round bowl of mixed flowers or a silk scarf draped over the mirror. In the guest room, leave one drawer partly open and drape a pair of long gloves or guest towels in the opening. Place a dish with peppermints or chocolate kisses on top of the dresser along with a small Bible, encouraging sweet, peaceful dreams.

The benefit to surface displays of art is that the family is less likely to place other clutter on the table or dresser. It actually keeps the room looking neater. So look around you. What creative tablescapes come to mind? Use your imagination, and some of the clutter will become a miniature work of art!

Simple Pleasures

- Take time today to sit in a chair you rarely enjoy. Enjoy the view from a new perch.
- Refinish or paint an old wooden school chair. Make it part of the children's playroom.
- Tie a ribbon on one chair at dinner. Whoever sits there gets to say the blessing!

Wisdom for Living

Fill my life with beauty, Lord.
I will arrange my days to serve and follow You.

On Display

I pray also that the eyes of your heart may be enlightened in order that you may know the hope to which he has called you, the riches of his glorious inheritance in the saints.

EPHESIANS 1:18

What do you most enjoy about the things you have gathered over the years? Do they hold special memories? Are they reminders of a certain time or a certain place you used to live? If you have a special collection, find a way to incorporate it into your home. Not only will your personality come shining through, but these material things will offer a sense of warmth and interest to your home on a more personal level.

Collections can be a challenge when it comes to decorating, but never fear. We can figure out something. How do you best show them off without looking cluttered—and a bit overwhelming? Grouping collections together works better than scattering them round the house. You might find it effective to let your collection set the theme for a room. For example, pink glassware might tie a room together by providing a color motif. A cookie jar collection would look great lined up across a mantel, or you could turn one or two of them into a lamp or table decoration.

Collections are just another way to share yourself with others. Like your spirit of loveliness, they will become an inheritance. Someday maybe you will be able to pass the collection on to your children.

Simple Pleasures

- Make a good memory today. Do something for yourself you have been putting off.
- Spend time in the Word. Focus on praises and prayers and make them your own.
- Meet a friend at a local art gallery. Praise God for His spirit of creativity and beauty.

Wisdom for Living

My earthly collections cannot compare to treasures stored in heaven, Lord. Let me enjoy such things but always with perspective to what matters most—You, my family, and my service to You.

Three Sweet Words

Let love and faithfulness never leave you; bind them around your neck, write them on the tablet of your heart. Then you will win favor and a good name in the sight of God and man.

PROVERBS 3:3-4

I love you. You are a sister in Christ and we share that faith in common. I can express that love because God first loved me. Me. I feel loved. Do you? Do those around you?

The Bible says: "Beloved, let us love one another, for love is from God" (1 John 4:7 NKJV). This is so true. There are times when even those closest to me are difficult to love, but I can show them God's love. Soon I feel the power of that obedience transform my feelings into pure, unconditional love.

When I say "I love you," it makes me feel good. It makes me realize I'm a giver and not just a taker. I often catch myself saying "I love you" as I hang up from talking to a friend or family member. You know what? After a while, they return the words. Use every opportunity to express those precious words. People who know they're loved have a cheerier outlook. There's a sparkle to their life. It's almost impossible not to like someone who says they love you. Make it your commitment today. Say "I love you!" to at least five people.

Simple Pleasures

* Tell yourself this morning that you are loved by the Giver of all life. Rest in that today.
* As someone who is unconditionally loved, think of one way you can make today count.
* Go to a floral shop and buy a mixed bouquet to enjoy all week long.

Wisdom for Living

*Father, love is such a gift. I share it with a small circle.
Let me embrace more people with Your love.*

A Prayer Notebook

Devote yourselves to prayer, keeping alert in it with an attitude of thanksgiving.

COLOSSIANS 4:2 NASB

How is your prayer life? Is it one of those areas where you have good intentions but just don't seem to get around to making it a daily habit? I've got just the tool you need—a prayer notebook. It's simple, and best of all it works! I so want you to infuse your life with prayer.

Get a three-ring binder, a set of tabs, and maybe 100 sheets of paper. Now you're ready for prayer requests. One tab could be family with a section for your spouse and for each child. Another can be the personal prayers between you and God. You'll also probably want tabs for finances, illness, and job-related requests. Make one for your pastor and church leaders, and another for missionaries. You can even include pictures. I like to divide the requests into days of the week.

It is such a wonderful feeling to pray over the life of your children. And when you see prayers answered and a child's life touched by God, you will become a real advocate for daily prayer. It does change your life.

The important things are to "keep it simple" and to use it every day. Ask God now to show you how you can seek first His kingdom. Make your own special appointment with God in prayer!

Simple Pleasures

- Spend some time this afternoon selecting a notebook or journal to use for prayer.
- Study a local travel guide and choose a special place to go and pray this week.
- When did you last spend 30 minutes in a hot bath relaxing? Today is your day!

Wisdom for Living

Thank You, Lord, for hearing my prayers.
You are my source of strength and hope. Oh, how fortunate
I am to be connected to my Creator through prayer.

Living from the Heart

Pay attention and listen to the sayings of the wise; apply your heart to what I teach.

PROVERBS 22:17

The older I become, the more I realize that living from my heart has value! Let's spend some mellow moments together this morning. No decorating, no organizing...just a heart-to-heart. I'd like to share what I have learned from my own time with God.

I want to live a life that's meaningful to my family and me. I want my decisions to be based on my Christian values. I don't want my decisions based on convenience, pressure, or selfishness. And in order to do that, I have to have some quiet times to read and think. Do you give yourself room and time to just be quiet? It is amazing how even 15 minutes of peace and reflection can renew your spirit.

When life becomes too hectic, when I'm constantly rushed, there's an inner disturbance that prevents me from making well-thought-out decisions. My personal growth grinds to a halt. My prayer is, "Father God, let me be more aware of the feelings of my heart." Here's a simple question for you today. How do you really want to live your life? Begin today to act on your answer to this question. In fact, for your next few quiet times or moments of devotion, I encourage you to revisit this question. Journal, pray, or just sit and ponder this question. Your priorities will become very clear as God's priorities become your own.

Simple Pleasures

- Go out and buy some new socks or nylons to replace your old ones.
- Make some old-fashioned sugar cookies to have with your personal snack time.
- Trust your heart today. Listen to your heart today.

Wisdom for Living

Lord, how should I live my life? I want my faith to guide my decisions. I want to be calm and clear thinking in situations so that I can follow Your priorities for my life.

Give It a Toss

There is a time for everything, and a season for every activity under heaven...a time to keep and a time to throw away.

ECCLESIASTES 3:1,6

Today let's determine we're going to throw away anything we don't need! This can be a painful process for some personality types, but I don't know a soul who doesn't feel better when they remove unnecessary baggage from their home. We all have it.

For example, those recipes, articles, school papers, old magazines, receipts, and expired coupons have to go. For items that are still timely and tempting to keep around awhile, choose five pieces and toss the rest into your trash bag.

Start with whatever clutter annoys you the most. Be sure you take advantage of today...a chance to really, really make life simpler for your family and yourself. Go through those drawers and closets where paper has accumulated and just start tossing. Even in this day of computers and storing information as data, we end up printing out a lot of interesting information. This really adds up. Get rid of it. Recycle that paper and find the desk you know exists beneath the piles.

When our lives are cluttered, often our hearts are cluttered and there's no room left over for the important things. So clear your environment and let your inner spirit rest.

Simple Pleasures

* Read Ecclesiastes 3:1-6 and reflect on God's timing for everything under heaven.
* Volunteer at a shelter or the organization you take your used clothing to.
* Play dress up from your own closet. Try on combinations you never dreamed of.

Wisdom for Living

The worry, anxiety, and selfish thoughts that fill my mind are clutter in my heart, Lord. I will clean my home to bring it order. And I will seek a pure mind and heart so that I have order within as well.

45

This Is Your Life

My son, do not forget my teaching, but keep my commands in your heart.

PROVERBS 3:1

One way to pass along your love and your values to your children is to pass on special memories to them. When our children graduated from high school, I prepared a "This Is Your Life" album for each of them. I bought scrapbooks and decorated the covers, and then I filled them with items from birth announcements to graduation pictures. There were report cards, hand-drawn pictures, invitations, photos of friends, and letters they'd written from camp. Even now they refer to their books for names and dates. They entertain their children with evidence that they were once children! And it provides them the opportunity to pass along a legacy.

If your children are young, this is the time to start gathering such memorabilia. Another good reason to get organized! Don't save every finger-painted picture, but certainly hold on to those that reflect their personality, their creative spirit, and their thoughtfulness. Record milestones with keepsakes like ticket stubs and recital programs.

As you can well imagine, one of my favorite verses is Hebrews 13:8, which says, "Jesus Christ is the same yesterday and today and forever." His presence in your home is a legacy that never fades.

Simple Pleasures

* Once a month, take a photo of your children doing something they enjoy.
* Share with your children what you learned from your parents.
* Revisit one of your childhood pleasures. Visit a swing set in the park and feel the wind.

Wisdom for Living

They grow up so fast, Lord. I want them to remember the many times we laughed and loved as a family. Let the heritage of their faith be evident in their reflections and memories.

Handwritten Treasures

> *The Word became flesh and made his dwelling among us. We have seen his glory, the glory of the One and Only, who came from the Father, full of grace and truth.*
>
> JOHN 1:14

I can well understand why people have told me that a loved-one's Bible—with underlined passages and notes scribbled in the margin—is a timeless treasure. I've made a point to leave my children that kind of personal, handwritten treasure from me. I'll pull out my stationery and tell them just how much I love them. I write about how excited I was when they were born. I relive favorite memories of them as children. I applaud their efforts to be good parents, and I tell them what a great job I think they're doing. The letters are my way of giving them my love and encouragement in tangible form.

While the power of oral history is great, a written account of a certain time or moment will also mean much to a child. Someday, you will not be around to remind them of special moments and how much their love meant to you as they grew up. Write them down and write from the heart. Maybe these are things you are not able to share out loud (though I hope you work toward that), but for now create a record that will stand the test of time.

Scripture is our example of this. God has given each of us His love and encouragement in tangible form. What a timeless treasure it is!

Simple Pleasures

- Write a letter to each of your children today. Tuck it away to deliver at a later time.
- If you go on a trip, send your children postcards to let them know what you saw that reminded you of them.
- Explain to your children the beauty of God's written Word.

Wisdom for Living

Your Word fills me with joy, Lord. I see Your heart and Your face through the Scriptures. I thank You that Your Word became flesh in the form of Jesus Christ.

Don't Let the Dust Settle

Watch yourselves closely so that you do not forget the things your eyes have seen or let them slip from your heart as long as you live. Teach them to your children and to their children after them.

Don't let those family heirlooms gather dust! Use special treasures. Maybe they are collections you started or items your mother or father passed along to you. Be sure they become part of your life so that they are truly enjoyed.

If I want to use an antique dresser scarf to line a tray, I just open a drawer in the kitchen because they're right there ready to use. I keep my collection of children's books on a shelf in the guest room where overnight guests can enjoy them. And in our house, the teacups and teaspoons and other tea items that make up my collection are simply everywhere. When the grandchildren come over, we drink tea from them. I truly believe children grow by being entrusted with treasures. We all do.

The things I cherish are better off when they're surrounded by everyday living. If you are too protective, it is much like having a guarded heart...life is not as full. I'm so much happier surrounded by beauty and memories. In other words, let yourself show.

Simple Pleasures

* Bring out a family treasure from storage, let it breathe, and place it somewhere to enjoy it.
* Ask your children what they consider to be treasures in your home.
* Polish your family silverware or add shine to an heirloom piece of furniture.

Wisdom for Living

Lord, You gave us faith so that we would embrace it and use it!
Let me apply this wisdom to all that I have.
Blessings are meant to be passed on.

March

THE GIFT OF LOVE

Friendship Tea

To love him with all your heart, with all your understanding and with all your strength, and to love your neighbor as yourself is more important than all burnt offerings and sacrifices.

Who are the friends you hold dear? Are there new friends you would like to introduce to old friends? A "friendship tea" is a great way to spend time with women who make a difference in your life.

But where to begin? Plan a menu that works best for you. Remember, we're trying to do it nice but keep it simple too! Set the table with fresh flowers from your garden. Bring out your best plates and make your table setting as beautiful as you can. Have several varieties of tea, maybe some cinnamon sticks for flavoring, scones and heavy cream, and soft music in the background. At one of my friendship teas I gave each lady a small candle. As I lit the candle of the person next to me, I shared a blessing: "Thank you for your loving friendship." We did that all around the table, each lady sharing from her heart. Believe me, it was a wonderful day. A "tissue time" to be sure!

This gathering will open up the hearts of the women you know. Sharing needs and joys with one another becomes a very enriching experience. Once you try this, you might discover that a tradition has been born.

Simple Pleasures

A friend is someone who reaches out for your hand…
and touches your heart.

—KATHLEEN GROVE

Wisdom for Living

Lord, please knit together the hearts of my friends.
May we learn to serve one another with kindness and friendship.

It's the Sharing

Surely goodness and love will follow me all the days of my life, and I will dwell in the house of the LORD forever.

PSALM 23:6

The gift of hospitality is one we can all adopt to make our home an inviting place for visitors, family, and friends. You want your house to be beautiful. You want it comfortable and cozy. Yet, in the end, what really matters is the sharing.

Before you become too caught up in elaborate details to get your home "just so" for discerning visitors, remember that the simplest gestures can extend the greatest sense of sharing. You can offer the warmth of a smile, a kind word, a place of shelter during an afternoon downpour, a prepared meal for a hungry guest.

Whatever you do to your walls and your windows, don't forget that the most wonderful adornment to your house is your spirit of hospitality and your willingness to share your home, your life, and your faith with others. You don't need to wait until everything's perfect. It never will be! After all, people live in your house. Something will always need repainting, recovering, or replacing. You'll always be wanting to add something here and take out something there. But share anyway. Love what you have and invite others in to share the bounty. Your home will always be its most beautiful when you stretch out your arms in welcome.

Simple Pleasures

- Use a facial mask today and sip lemonade while you wait for it to dry.
- Set out some new potpourri that smells like spring flowers.
- Repair an item of clothing you miss having in your wardrobe.

Wisdom for Living

Lord, help me remember that my home at this very moment and in every state of cleanliness is a place to express the gift of hospitality. Thank You for the blessing of a home.

Where Do I Display It?

Show the wonder of your great love, you who save by your right hand those who take refuge in you from their foes.

PSALM 17:7

When you have a collection of any size, it is often because the theme is one which brings you pleasure. Chances are, this collection will also bring pleasure into your home's style if you choose to share and display it. Do you know right where you would arrange your collection? It only takes a few minutes to survey your favorite rooms and decide where those vintage books, teaspoons, or handwoven linens would add a touch of personality.

Don't forget the obvious! The simplest place to put your collection is out in the open. Stack your treasured books and Bibles on shelves and lamp tables. Spread quilts on your beds. Always group collections for display. Place a small crowd of teddy bears in the corner. Line a parade of glass bottles along a windowsill. Crowd small toys together on a table. Use your imagination. One creative woman transformed an unused fireplace into a cozy den for stuffed animals. Arrange baby clothes and favorite toys in a shadow box.

Each time you pass one of these special, unique decorations, your spirits will be lifted. It's fun to discover how the heart of your home can be a ministry to you, your family, and your friends.

Simple Pleasures

* Place a new candle in your bedroom. Light it ten minutes before you retire for the evening.
* Sift through the reading material on your nightstand. Clear out anything you have read.
* Choose one piece of furniture to use for a purpose other than what it was made for.

Wisdom for Living

*My home is Your home, Father. I pray that it is
a place that is pleasing to You, filled with love, laughter,
and special treasures of the heart.*

Making Guests Feel Welcome

Share with God's people who are in need. Practice hospitality.

ROMANS 12:13

Have you ever been truly welcomed? It is such a warm, comfortable feeling. You are taken care of, loved, and even a bit pampered. What a gift to give to the guests who enter your home.

There are easy, simple ways to share this feeling with your visitors. For a dinner guest, a tiny gift by their plate—a small address book, a pen, a powder puff, a book, a small vase of flowers—will fill their appetite for friendship. For overnight guests, invest in extra pillows, blankets, and other bedding. Store them in pillowcases to keep them fresh and dust-free. Tie a silk ribbon around a towel set and your guest will know those towels are laid out just for them. When space is limited, prepare a child's room for the guest, complete with a written invitation from the child to help your guest feel at home in the room. Give your child the "privilege" of camping out in the living room. The result: An adventure for your child and welcome privacy for your guest.

Place photos of yourself with your guest on the bedside table in the guest room. What a fun surprise! And what a nice touch to have a devotional book next to the lamp. It tells your guest, "We love you and you're welcome in our home!"

Simple Pleasures

- Practice hospitality in a new way today. Seek out opportunities to show love to others.
- Write a welcome blessing. Read the book of Psalms for inspiration.
- Think of some things you enjoy when you are a guest. Implement those in your home.

Wisdom for Living

Lord, I see Your face in the faces of my guests.
May I always share my home with a willing spirit
and a kindness that matches Your own.

Custom Tailored

My soul thirsts for God, for the living God. When can I go and meet with God?

PSALM 42:2

When you first became a Christian, what impressed you most about the love of Christ? What characteristic of our Lord has stayed with you through the good times and the difficult times? This shows how important a first impression really is. It sets the tone of our relationship with someone.

The best kind of first impression is a personal one. It reflects your tastes, and it says a lot about your caring. We have a little chalkboard right outside our kitchen door. We change the greeting depending on who's coming over. Sometimes it says something like, "Christine is almost 13!" Our granddaughter loved that! Another welcoming touch can be a bench outside the door. To me, a bench just calls out to friends to sit down and relax a bit. It's kind of like the old porch swing, which I think was a great invention. It's inviting, friendly. It says, "Come and sit and let's enjoy one another." Whatever you use to greet your guests, let it be personal and cheerful. And let it be as beautiful as possible. It could help bring about a lasting, eternal friendship.

Let your home be a sanctuary where you, your family, and visitors come to meet the Lord.

Simple Pleasures

- Sing a song out loud today. Start your morning with good cheer.
- When was the last time you skipped? Try skipping down your hallway.
- Start a guest book if you do not yet have one. It will be a record of great fellowship.

Wisdom for Living

Dear Father, I pray that the first impression I make on everyone I meet is one that represents Your goodness and Your love for that person.

Family Hospitality

I love the house where you live, O LORD, the place where your glory dwells.

PSALM 26:8

Have you heard that it is easier to be nicer to strangers than to family members? Is it because we are on our best behavior with visitors? Or is it because we feel our efforts will be most appreciated by a guest?

Why not treat your family as guests? You will be amazed at what happens when you take the time to greet your own family with that special "I'm excited to see you" welcome. Why not stroll out to meet your spouse at the end of a hard day? Have snacks and drinks in the fridge for a little family "happy hour" before the evening starts. The same is true for goodbyes. Occasionally go for a big hug and a personal escort out the door. Every once in awhile, a little wrapped gift or a note slipped into a briefcase or backpack can start a day off with an extra bit of sunshine and love.

When a guest comes over, isn't it true that you try to serve a meal that is their preference? Select an evening and assign one family member to choose the dinner or dessert you will prepare. This one especially is an easy way to have each child and your spouse feel extra special. Do one of these dinners a month and make a night of it complete with a board game or movie rental of the "guest's" choosing.

The simple message in all of these efforts is: "I really am glad you're here, and I just can't wait until you come back!"

Simple Pleasures

- Spend time with an old family Bible. Pray about your family and future generations.
- Ask your husband what you could help him with this weekend.
- Let a child pick a place for the family to go to breakfast together.

Wisdom for Living

Lord, serving the family You have given me is a joy.
Bless each of them and help us all to treat one another kindly.

With Fresh Eyes

He welcomed us to his home and for three days entertained us hospitably.

Acts 28:7

Proverbs 24:3 says: "By wisdom a house is built, and through understanding it is established." The wisdom of the Lord creates the foundation for your "house" and your household. And through the nurturing and understanding of God's love and His ways, you will see your family grow and become established.

Implementing that "understanding" in a home can be as easy as walking out the front door, turning around, and coming right back in. There. What do you see that is welcoming? What expresses the love and knowledge of your family and your Lord?

With fresh eyes, you will see ways to make your home inviting. I have a few starter ideas. Keep a guest book for visitors to sign. Your entranceway is a great place for a "love wall." Group all the plaques and pictures people have given you as gifts or use that space for candid family photos. Choose a small area at the front of your house for something green or growing! Prepare a welcome bag or basket for guests. Or have parting gifts. An instant photo of the guest in your home will remind your visitors that they are a part of your family.

Do this fresh-look check every once in awhile. Pay attention to what catches your eye and, even more important, what catches your heart!

Simple Pleasures

* Invite local family members to stay overnight sometime. Celebrate them!
* Have a sleepover for some of *your* friends. Watch movies, talk, laugh.
* Buy yourself some new slippers. Fuzzy ones. Or bright blue ones.

Wisdom for Living

*God, I choose to build my house on Your wisdom and follow
Your example of giving and reaching out. Today I will look
at my home and my life with fresh eyes. What is pleasing to You?*

Have Some Tea

My purpose is that they may be encouraged in heart and united in love, so that they may have the full riches of complete understanding.

COLOSSIANS 2:2

The old-fashioned tea party has become the "in thing" for entertaining! Don't be intimidated by hosting one if it is your first time. I think the word "party" sometimes implies big responsibility. I am talking about making tea, creating a bit of ambience, and having a couple friends or neighbors over. Simple. Fun. Refreshing.

Serve your tea in the part of your house that most delights your senses—it could be the living room, the kitchen, even the porch. Go outdoors, if you can. Have fresh flowers on your table—a bunch of baby's breath looks so elegant. A collection of unmatched teapots, spoons, cups, and plates has a special charm of its own. Pay attention to presentation. Use flowers, herbs, and vegetables to make beautiful garnishes. Arrange foods in pleasing combinations. Let graciousness and love abound in every way.

You'll enjoy teatime more if you feel as beautiful as your home and table. At your party, enjoy something else that's back in style—hats! A hat is just right for a tea.

Simple Pleasures

- Place some new bath gels and lotions in a wicker basket for your use.
- Buy some grapes or other fruit and enjoy it with sharp cheddar cheese.
- Make a dinner reservation for you and your husband this week.

Wisdom for Living

Lord, whom can I serve today?
Who would be encouraged by a bit of tea with a friend?

The Royal Treatment

So in everything, do to others what you would have them do to you.

MATTHEW 7:12

Hospitality thrives in the simplest of settings. It's a matter of opening your life to others. Giving them the best you have to offer. We want all of our guests to have the royal treatment.

How would you like to stay in the "Princess Room"? This royal-sounding name always amuses our guests. It also paints a picture of how we want our guests to feel—pampered, appreciated, and loved. Hospitality is so much more than entertaining. In fact, the Bible tells us to practice hospitality (Romans 12:13). You don't need elaborate preparations, just personal touches. A really nice touch is a handy basket of basic overnight needs so that if your guests forgot any items or perhaps someone decides last minute to stay over, they will still feel at home. These items are easy to gather: new toothbrushes, toothpaste, little hotel shampoos, lotions, even dental floss.

We love to welcome guests for a meal, an evening, or just a cup of tea. And we enjoy extending the invitation for people to spend a night or two in our Princess Room. When a guest feels accepted and wanted, rather than a disruption or bother, their happiness is written across their face in a smile. To us, this is sharing our lives on a deeper level.

Simple Pleasures

Welcome is what reflects God's spirit
of love, joy, and happiness.

—EMILIE BARNES

Wisdom for Living

Dear Father, I want to share my life.
When I extend an invitation to a person,
I want to fully welcome them. Let it be a time of friendship
and joy for me, my family, and our special guest.

New Gifts from Old

Just as Christ was raised from the dead through the glory of the Father, we too may live a new life.

ROMANS 6:4

Lost-and-found treasure! They're the source for some of the most creative and memorable gifts. Just think how the Lord transformed your lost soul into a heart bound for heaven. Let this treasure be a source of inspiration for you.

A gift you make yourself will be unique and appreciated. Frame a montage of childhood keepsakes and give it to a grown child. Have an old ring reset with a new stone and give it to your teenager. Antique buttons are so popular. Use them in a collage or to decorate clothing. Using ink stamps, make monogrammed stationery for a friend and give her ten sheets with an old-fashioned fountain pen. Save satin and lace to cover a wedding album, make a pillow, or trim a baby dress. Use pieces of broken china to make unique gifts. For a friend's birthday, give her an item like a vase or piece of china made in the year she was born. Surprise someone with a gift of vintage clothing—a hat, a camisole, or even a dress. And vintage handbags—what a great gift.

The idea is to pass along your own unique gift of love. Such thoughtful gifts are really just ways to package kindness!

Simple Pleasures

- Send a card to a friend just to tell them how much they mean to you.
- Surprise a single friend with flowers at work to brighten her day.
- Help a friend learn a new skill on her computer.

Wisdom for Living

Gifts of love are easy to make or discover, Lord.
When it comes to gifts, help me to choose the perfect expression
of love for each special person I want to bless.

Passing the Torch

I will instruct you and teach you in the way you should go; I will counsel you and watch over you.

PSALM 32:8

Passing on the torch of womanhood is so much more than teaching sewing or how to clean a house, do laundry, cook, or arrange flowers. To me, passing on the legacy of being a woman is most of all the teaching of values, caring for others, and nurturing a godly atmosphere in my home and life.

The time we spend teaching our daughters—and our sons—about the joys and responsibilities of womanhood will provide benefits for generations to come. And we teach best by what we are, not just by what we say. That's why I pray, "Lord, may the love of Christ permeate my heart and life and spread its gentle fragrance into the lives and hearts of those I meet each day."

How has your heart been nourished by another woman? What did you learn from her that you wish to pass along? Think about how you wish to show Christ's love to others, especially to a younger woman. If you do not have an opportunity right now, pray for one and start watching for God's response. When we invest in the lives of other women, we build the kingdom of God.

Simple Pleasures

- Call or write a letter of thanks for a woman who has mentored you in some way.
- Have a girls' night out with your daughters or nieces.
- Use your home as a place for young women to gather for a study or reading group.

Wisdom for Living

Lord, I want to share my love for You with other women.
How can I serve someone today? I pray Your light
will shine brightly on those I meet.

Let's Share a Meal

These things I remember as I pour out my soul: how I used to go with the multitude, leading the procession to the house of God, with shouts of joy and thanksgiving among the festive throng.

PSALM 42:4

Are you ready to offer some good old-fashioned hospitality? Reach out to those around you in small and big ways. Look for opportunities to serve others in the name of the Lord.

Let's be thankful for what we have and make the best of it to glorify God. Inviting someone over for dinner can provide a bright spot for a stressed-out friend or someone who's just in need of some stillness in their life. God says we're to have a cheerful heart in our hospitality. Regardless of how small a home you have, you can share it with someone else. Invite a new friend home after church for a simple lunch. Hospitality is the practice of welcoming, sheltering, and feeding—with no thought of personal gain. It means setting aside time for fellowship and being flexible so you can make yourself available, even at the spur of the moment.

We tend to think of hospitality as a huge effort or a planned event with invitations sent out. Hospitality is meant for everyday living. Hospitality is what our heart offers those people who come into our lives either for just a moment or for a long stay. Show your heart and the Lord's heart with three people today. Bless you!

Simple Pleasures

- Host a neighborhood family for dinner.
- Plan a night to serve take-out pizza and take a break from the kitchen!
- Have an old-fashioned malt or shake night at your house for the kids.

Wisdom for Living

I want a giving heart, Lord. Guide me in reaching out to three people today. You know their needs. Help me reach these needs with the simple expression of hospitality.

Let's Sparkle!

Arise, shine, for your light has come, and the glory of the LORD rises upon you.

ISAIAH 60:1

As women of God we have a wonderful opportunity to let our lives sparkle! We are so lucky. Enjoy this opportunity to the fullest by incorporating a few of these ideas into your day.

Get one of those lovely blank books and commit to praying on paper for at least six weeks. Try it, you may not want to stop! Frame a family photo and put it where you get ready for the day. Pray for your family while you do your makeup or dry your hair. Be on the lookout for ways to obey God by serving others. Look for ways to turn your everyday activities into prayers of thanksgiving. Ask God to use those mundane tasks you have to do as tasks for His glory. When you return calls, pray briefly for each person. Ask God to bless his or her life through you.

You will soon see the shine and sparkle that fills your daily life. You are polishing gems of great value through these simple acts...you are caring about the hearts of others.

Simple Pleasures

- Pray a new prayer. Begin with a different phrase and see where it leads your heart.
- Send someone a postcard saying you are praying for them specifically.
- Make a bookmark out of fabric pieces, beads, or ribbon. Get creative.

Wisdom for Living
Lord, a prayer life is such a blessing.
I want Your light to shine all day in my home and in my life.
Help me to see every opportunity I have to pray.

The First Thing You See

Taste and see that the LORD is good; blessed is the man who takes refuge in him.

PSALM 34:8

As guests enter your home, how does your house welcome them? Find ways to be a gracious host by creating a carefree area for visitors to get settled in no time. You will discover that these tips also create a warm atmosphere for your family.

Once the door is open, the basics should be there—a place to wipe feet, a place to hang coats and hats, a mirror to check hair when coming in from the rain. The entranceway sets the mood and sends a message about the whole house. Paint the area a soft, inviting color that is a complement to the larger area's hue. Place a framed photo of the family at eye level so your visitors will be greeted by smiles right away. A neat foyer with a shiny floor and sparkling mirror says, "This house is orderly and peaceful." A cozy apartment living room with plump cushions, soft music, and lots of candles says, "Come on in—let's get to know you."

And of course the smell of something wonderful on the stove is an unmistakable welcome. I know of more than one person who's sold her house quickly by popping a loaf of bread dough into the oven before prospective buyers showed up! Simple, but inviting.

Simple Pleasures

- Play "I Spy" with your children while driving.
- Hide a shiny button somewhere for a little one to find. Have a treasure hunt.
- Have a basket of spare umbrellas, mittens, and hats that can wander away forever.

Wisdom for Living

Dear Father, let all visitors enter my home with ease.
May their hearts feel welcomed even before they hear a spoken greeting.

Don't Forget the Candles

Whoever can be trusted with very little can also be trusted with much.

In honor of making small things matter, let's spend time today in the bathroom with some simple ideas for making this space as nice as possible. Often this room is left to be a mismatch of looks or colors. Bringing the color and design schemes together will unify the overall look. This doesn't mean a cookie-cutter format. Go with your original tastes and style even here. The small space will actually feel larger and more spacious if you treat it as a regular room.

I've seen some wonderful, creative ideas for decorating bathrooms. One featured a lovely hooked rug instead of the standard issue bath mat. One had family photos (copies, not originals) in antique oval frames. And another treated the tank as a little curio shelf with a cloth drape, photograph, and a pretty plant. Others have used china bowls to hold tiny soaps and a pretty basket for magazines. If you have small children, decorate the wooden step they use when washing their hands. And place a towel rack that matches your other ones at their level for easy hand drying.

In other words, the bathroom doesn't have to be the predictable matching mat and cover! Have fun decorating this most private of rooms to make it lovely and interesting. And don't forget the candles!

Simple Pleasures

- Get a new bathroom rug to add a new color, or add a shower curtain in a new style.
- Place a lamp on the bathroom counter. Use a low wattage bulb for a calm feel.
- Melt down pieces of old candles and create a new one. All you need is a new wick.

Wisdom for Living

Today, Father, I will make even the smallest tasks acts of joy and reflections of my thankfulness for all You do in my life.

Oh, No—A Teenager!

The fruit of the Spirit is love, joy, peace, patience, kindness, goodness, faithfulness, gentleness and self-control.

GALATIANS 5:22-23

What happened to those sweet young children who used to live in our homes? They became teenagers, that's what happened! I pray these few simple survival tips for those teen years will offer encouragement as well as guidance.

Remember your children are God's children, and He loves them unconditionally. They won't always be in this phase, I promise you! Don't take everything they say or do personally. This is difficult because they can be hurtful or careless with their words at this age. Keep in mind they also have a foundation of love because you raised them that way. They will get back to that, eventually.

Accept them, and they will be more likely to accept themselves. Try to keep your sense of humor. Fortunately (at least in most cases), children will not become the adults they are as teenagers. Whew! Having teenagers will definitely improve your prayer life. Having a teenager will also make you a better parent and a better person. Hug that teenager of yours today. Let her know how much you love her! Let him know how proud you are of him.

Simple Pleasures

- Train up your child in the fruit of the Spirit.
- Practice these virtues as you communicate with your child.
- When talking to your teen is difficult, show your love every way you can.

Wisdom for Living

*Thank You for my teenagers, Lord,
or the children who are going to someday be teenagers!
I will draw my strength from You, and I will never stop
showing my children love and acceptance.*

65

Speech Patterns

> My tongue will speak of your righteousness and of your praises all day long.
>
> PSALM 35:28

Our children participated in adult conversation from the very beginning. Bob and I wanted them to feel comfortable around our adult friends. Many times they would just listen, but as they grew older they entered in with feelings and opinions. It was during these times that we taught manners, thoughtfulness, and courtesies. No question was too dumb or thoughtless. We had a lot of laughs with each other, but not *at* the expense of another member of the family. If your child has not been involved up to this point, try to include them in the next adult gathering. Have it be in a way that is comfortable. Perhaps they could be the official greeter so that they have one-on-one interaction right away and can feel comfortable talking to people later. Maybe they will just join you and your adult friends for the meal. The dining room table is a great place to teach children to interact. This is one thing we've lost from the past...many families no longer eat a meal together around the family table.

I think an important concept needs to reappear in our families: Good old-fashioned talking with one another. To have an impact on our children, we have to spend time with them! It's so simple.

Simple Pleasures

- Practice manners in your home with your child. They will learn respect for others.
- Host a tea for little ones and teach them mealtime manners.
- Post a list of affirming words on a bulletin board as a reminder to speak kindly.

Wisdom for Living

Lord, I know communication leads to relationships that are meaningful and lasting. I pray I will create good communication with my children and that I will teach them to do the same throughout their lives.

Too Good to Believe

I want to share with you a story…a true story about the help of friends. It is hard to believe, but just read on. I was staying in the home of a couple who was moving in two days. As I looked around, I noticed nothing was packed. I finally asked my friend about it because I was becoming a bit anxious on her behalf. I was thinking of all the things I would be doing right now instead of spending time with a friend.

"Oh, no," she explained, "I don't pack at all. On moving day there will be 20 to 30 men from the church. They'll pack and move the entire household to our new home where the women are scrubbing, painting, and wallpapering. By dinnertime, food will be brought in for everyone. Friends helping friends." This same couple told me that when a woman became pregnant, ten ladies in one afternoon sewed an entire maternity wardrobe for her to wear and enjoy.

What? Such wonderful examples of extraordinary kindnesses. I was absolutely overwhelmed. And just think how the recipients felt. They were abundantly blessed by God's love pouring out on them through others.

Simple Pleasures

- Think about the evidence of God's overwhelming love in your life.
- Do you know someone who needs a touch of extraordinary kindness? Make a list and choose a person to help this week.
- Spend your devotion time this week praising God for people who have shown you His love.

Wisdom for Living

Lord, Your mercy is abundant and so tender. The goodness of friends and strangers makes me rejoice and call You "Father."

Good for You

Then you and your household shall eat there in the presence of the LORD your God and rejoice.

DEUTERONOMY 14:26

Landmark birthdays, graduations, a wedding. Can you remember those days without remembering the special friends who shared them with you? I can't. All the more reason to plan a special day to commemorate a special occasion. And center that day around a tea. It's something different for a wedding shower, an anniversary celebration, a birthday, or honoring a special achievement.

When you invite guests to the tea, make sure you inform them of the party's purpose. Maybe have a blessing or teatime prayer written on the invitations to set the tone for the celebration. Consider a little testimonial, a speech from the guest of honor, and definitely a "toast with tea cups"! The point is to make it a big deal. Make it memorable for the one you're celebrating.

Pay attention to any milestones your friends or family members will be reaching in the near future. A new job or a job promotion. Going back to school. The completion of a major project. There are so many reasons to celebrate with those around you. The biggest is that they are special to you. Find any excuse you can to surround them with love.

And when you do, take lots of pictures and be sure to get a group shot as a beautiful reminder of a special day!

Simple Pleasures

* Make a batch of cookies...the kind *you* like...and enjoy them with milk.
* Have a personal tea to celebrate Your Lord! Tell Him why you celebrate Him.
* Choose a goal that you plan to reach and celebrate this year.

Wisdom for Living

I choose to celebrate the people in my life.
Lord, I will seek ways to honor
my special friends and my loving family.

A Little Recipe Book

Give thanks to the LORD, for he is good; his love endures forever.

1 CHRONICLES 16:34

Something that lasts! It's important to all of us, isn't it? I want to encourage you to notice the simple treasures in your life. Just when you think your life is a bit bland or too routine, you'll discover it holds many amazing treasures.

Lovingly prepared cooking can be a handcrafted treasure! It's almost a lost art these days. The actual food quickly becomes a memory, but the recipes and skills survive to be passed down from generation to generation.

One of my favorite treasures—and most used, I might add—is a little recipe book Bob's mother compiled for me and my sister-in-law. In it are all the recipes our husbands love best. I've long cherished her generosity. She was giving away something she could have kept to herself. She was giving me the power to nurture and cherish her son. In the process, she was also giving me a piece of herself. A simple gift became a simple, lasting act of love.

Simple Pleasures

- Create a list of your favorite foods.
- Plan a night this week to serve your husband's favorite meal.
- If it has been a hard week for you and your spouse, order a take-out meal from your favorite restaurant. Serve it by candlelight, even if it is pizza!

Wisdom for Living

Dear Father, we find treasures when we look to the blessings You have given. May I always see the treasures in my life.

A Home of Love

And we, who with unveiled faces all reflect the Lord's glory, are being transformed into his likeness with ever-increasing glory, which comes from the Lord, who is the Spirit.

2 CORINTHIANS 3:18

Does your home reflect love? Let it shine! The beloved Christian poet Amy Carmichael wrote: "If I'm inconsiderate about the comfort of others, or their feelings, or even their little weaknesses; if I am careless about their little hurts and miss opportunities to smooth their way; if I make the sweet running of household wheels more difficult to accomplish, then I know nothing of Calvary love." It's almost impossible not to feel loved when you're in a setting that says, "I love you." The refrigerator door that's always open for tiny hands to check out its contents. The adults who find flowers and soothing music that relax stress and tension.

What says "love" to you? Fill your home with the pleasures that give you so much joy. Extra blankets. Framed paintings of flowers. Growing plants. A cross on the wall.

Take a close look at your surroundings. Does your home reflect God's love and provision? Pray this prayer, "Father God, show me how I can share Your love in my home. Amen."

Simple Pleasures

- Bring some fabric swatches into your room to see how colors add new shine.
- Spend some time with a favorite magazine. Take notes on what catches your eye.
- Wash the dishes by candlelight tonight. It will soothe your senses and your home.

Wisdom for Living

Love should be given to all who enter my home.
Show me how to spread Your love to my family
and to anyone who visits this house, Lord.

April

SPRINGING INTO SPRING

I'll Do It Tomorrow

You need to persevere so that when you have done the will of God, you will receive what he has promised.

HEBREWS 10:36

If you're a procrastinator, getting into motion can be frustrating! I empathize with you. Do you need a push? While this might not sound like a friendly offer, it really is. I would love to help you move toward the completion of a project or the attainment of a goal. Let's work together. Maybe these hints will help get you started.

Break down overwhelming tasks into small ones. Face the tasks you have to do right in the eye. Ignoring them doesn't make them go away. Make a commitment to a friend, and then ask him or her to hold you accountable for getting started. Here's the tip I like best. Give yourself a reward. Choose something simple that will bring you pleasure when you are done—perhaps taking time to read a good book or have a coffee date with a friend. Maybe you are longing to sign up for a women's weekend retreat with your church. It's easier to be away from home if you feel things are in order there.

By all means, give yourself deadlines. Color-code the due date on your calendar if you have to. And *be decisive!* Have the courage to act. Don't be crippled by the "what if's"…the "I'm gonnas"…the "I want's"—make something happen!

Simple Pleasures

- Start small. Decide on one thing you promise yourself you will do this week.
- Give yourself the reward of a chocolate wafer and milk this afternoon.
- Is the sun shining? Sit on the porch and read the paper.

Wisdom for Living

Give me the courage to reach my goals, Lord.
I want to be a person who grows each new day as You provide me with lessons to learn and successes to experience.

More Time for Yourself

Create in me a pure heart, O God, and renew a steadfast spirit within me.

PSALM 51:10

Do you want more time for yourself and your family? Of course you do! But how? One way is to get all those little jobs out of the way. First of all, make a "to do" list and be sure to set some manageable deadlines. You might want to use a timer for bite-sized tasks, like writing a note, cleaning a bathroom, or changing the bed. This way you are sure to watch out for interruptions and distractions. If you are baking or cooking during the day, use the cooking increments as project timelines. Allow 30 minutes to straighten the living room. Forty-five minutes to round up laundry and sweep the floor. When you multitask, it seems as though you are doing two things at once. You will feel invincible.

Here is a simple idea that can really help: use your answering machine. Learn to say no until you've completed what you've set out to do. Ask your family to help you. And be sure you reward yourself. When you have crossed off one or more of the items on your list, have lunch with a friend or sit down with a cup of tea and your Bible.

Simple Pleasures

- Make spaghetti sauces, taco meat, chili, and freeze them in meal-size containers.
- Encourage your children to help with dinner by using those pre-made ingredients!
- Bake large batches of your family's favorite muffins. Freeze them so your family can enjoy homemade treats on the way to school or work.

Wisdom for Living

More time is a precious gift. I want more time for my family and for You, God. Help me to see the ways in which I waste time.

Are You a Pack Rat?

You are already clean because of the word I have spoken to you. Remain in me, and I will remain in you.

JOHN 15:3-4

Are things collecting on top of your refrigerator, counters, end tables, and bookshelves? Do you often say, "It might come in handy—someday?" You may be a pack rat. If you have a difficult time deciding whether to throw something or store it, put those items into a box or baggie and put the container in the garage. If the box or bag sits for several months untouched, it's a sure indication to either give those items away or throw them away. "Out of sight, out of mind" is a good saying to remember. If you are a pack rat to the core, you might want to call on the help of a good friend. Plan a tough love cleaning session some afternoon and tell your friend to really challenge you on each item. "Do you really need this? Want this? Use this?" If you verbalize the truth that you haven't worn a certain sweater in five years, it makes the tossing that much easier.

Purging, cleaning, and ordering your home might feel a bit painful during the process, but I guarantee you will feel lighter, happier, and less tied down to material things after you do this. It is surprisingly freeing.

So throw away and give away. If you're going to be a pack rat, at least be an organized one!

Simple Pleasures

* Clean out your junk drawer and make room for information you want on hand.
* Keep a box of red licorice in the kitchen for an after-cleaning treat.
* Sip a diet soda or cup of tea once your big projects are done for the day.

Wisdom for Living

*I think someone else can make use of these items, Lord.
Help me give myself and my family breathing room
by lessening our ties to material possessions.*

Teach Your Children About Money

Watch your life and doctrine closely. Persevere in them, because if you do, you will save both yourself and your hearers.

1 TIMOTHY 4:16

Providing for your child is such an important part of parenting. It is also a reflection of God's provision for you, His child. Accept the responsibility with gratitude and with wisdom. One way to provide for children is to teach them life skills to match their level of responsibility. One of these skills is money management. If that scares you a little, you might need a refresher course yourself. These tips will help the entire family.

Bob and I incorporated these basic ideas to help our children get a good handle on money. Start with an allowance—it's a great way for teaching children how to budget, save, give, and make their own decisions. As parents, model the proper use of credit. Enough said? Teach your children how to save. It's difficult, but what an asset saving will be later on in their life. Encourage your children to help you budget for the family finances. It's real-world experience. And be sure to show them how to give to the Lord.

Here's the biggest lesson—teach them that money doesn't reflect love. A hug, a smile, or time spent together is much more valuable than money! When this is learned, they will discover that a person's worth has nothing to do with how much money they make. God does not care if we own stock options and a house in the Hamptons. He does care that we are good stewards of all we possess.

Simple Pleasures

- Get a fun bank for your child to use as a savings account or as his "giving away" fund.
- Teach children the joy of service by planning family volunteer adventures.
- Give a neighbor mom a break by inviting her children over for an early dinner.

Wisdom for Living

O God, saving for a rainy day is a lost art. Guide me as I model godly life principles for my children. Help me to recognize each person I meet as a person of great value, created in Your image.

Garage Sale Specialists

Behold, I will create new heavens and a new earth. The former things will not be remembered, nor will they come to mind.

ISAIAH 65:17

Are you either a garage sale specialist or a wannabe? Do you look at your boxes of "stuff" and think "someday I am really going to do it"? Well, I would love nothing better than to help you set one up. Garage sales are easy. All they take is a little advance planning.

Set the date and get out your ad to the community. And remember, never include your phone number. Make your signs with heavy cardboard or brightly colored posterboard. Get the kids involved.

Keep it simple. Just "Garage Sale," your address and street name are all you need. Make sure to put your signs in prominent locations. Then organize, organize, organize—and display the items in categories. Set your prices with stick-on labels or stickers. Have kids help with the stickers. Assign an adult as the cashier. Make sure all purchases go through that one person. Decide how low you will go on prices.

Do you have small items that you would love to pass along to others but are not sure if they will sell? Give them away. That's right, offer a free item from the giveaway box with every purchase. Or if your child has a few toys to give away, let your young visitors choose an item while their parents take their time looking around.

And make the time count! At the end of the day, take time out for a hot bath and a chance to relax!

Simple Pleasures

* Think of cleaning and getting rid of "stuff" as putting your home on a diet.
* Let neighbors know about your sale and see if they want to host a table too.
* Offer to help an elderly neighbor organize their garage or closets.

Wisdom for Living

When I come to You, Lord, with my burdens, You clean house.
You sweep away my sins, You get rid of my junk.
And You pay for it with Your Son's life.

Review Your Spending Habits

He must manage his own family
well and see that his children obey
him with proper respect.

<blockquote>1 Timothy 3:4</blockquote>

No matter how hard I shop for an item, the day after I buy it inevitably it goes on sale. But there are ways you can have more money to meet your bills. For example, carry only enough cash with you for that day's needs. You won't spend it if you don't have it with you. Shop the sales. Don't buy lottery tickets. The average lottery ticket buyer spends about $250 a year and wins nothing. Just think of all the ways you could use that money more wisely or even for more fun for your family.

Cut back on eating out. If the fun is to go out as a family and celebrate, eat a simple dinner at home and go out for a nice dessert. The evening will still feel special and you will have saved bundles. Watch that daily latté—it can cost you a fortune! Save them for a treat. Savor nice coffee when you are meeting a friend or schedule half an hour during a busy day when you could really use time at the coffee shop with the newspaper.

People with poor money management almost always have poor spending habits. Change your habits, and I guarantee that you will find your financial status and your lifestyle upgraded. The money will then be there for the really special purchases instead of two-dollar, five-dollar, and even ten-dollar spur-of-the-moment whims.

When you have to ask "where did all the money go?" at the end of each month, be sure you can feel good about the answer.

Simple Pleasures

- Cut out something useless from your budget. Decide how to spend this savings on something worthwhile.
- Start that change jar. You will be surprised how quickly coins add up to helpful cash.
- Encourage your child to begin the practice of tithing.

Wisdom for Living

Waste not, want not. I will watch the way I treat money.
Let it never become a stumbling block for me, Lord.

Getting Bunched In

If you have that "bunched in" problem at your house—join the club! Let's take a look at managing your stuff...the clutter that is taking over space you could be using for better purposes.

One thing that might help you is a rule at our home about abundance. Simply stated: "One comes in and one goes out." After every purchase we give away or sell a like item. This practice also teaches children that balance is better than striving to accumulate items. Adults can learn the same lesson. This means that after every Christmas, you will need to really focus on giving away to others. This practical idea becomes a wonderful holiday tradition.

Have an annual garage sale or participate in a neighborhood sale. Make sure a percentage of the sale goes to a good charity. Here's another strategy that's very effective. Bob and I informed our loved ones that we don't want any more gifts that take up space—or that have to be dusted. At this stage of our lives, we prefer consumable items. And I know parents who asked guests not to bring gifts for their small children's birthdays. When those toys start piling up and your child is overwhelmed with choices, it might be time to get creative with a child's clutter as well.

Remember, life isn't based on your possessions. Keep your life simple.

Simple Pleasures

* Get rid of items in each room that you don't use. They only create clutter in your home.
* When busy schedules get busier, let your Crock-Pot do the cooking.
* Keep a box of baking soda in both the refrigerator and freezer.

Wisdom for Living

A simple lifestyle suits my trust in You, Lord.
May I never get caught up in the need for things
when I have so many richer pursuits before me—prayer,
family, obedience to You, and spiritual growth.

Storage Solutions

I press on toward the goal to win the prize for which God has called me heavenward in Christ Jesus.

PHILIPPIANS 3:14

Can I offer you some simple solutions for your storage problems? Most everyone has a storage problem, by the way. It just takes a little creativity and solution-oriented focus to eliminate this problem. Better yet, eliminate some of your stuff! But in the meanwhile, seek multipurpose pieces of furniture which offer space and style for a room.

One of my favorite pieces of furniture is a little cabinet I bought at a garage sale. It's long and low with doors in front. We use it as a table behind our sofa, and have placed a little lamp and an antique scale on top. It's also wonderful for storing tablecloths and napkins. Whenever we're in an antique store, we're on the lookout for such pieces. Over the years, Bob and I have collected an oak icebox that stores our crystal, a Hoosier cabinet that proudly displays teapots and teacups, and a variety of wardrobes and bookcases that offer storage as well as decorate our home.

When placing pieces like this in your house or apartment, think of the impact they will have on a large or small room. It can be dramatic and wonderful. These pieces we have brought into our home over time all look so beautiful—who's to know they're also helping the work of this household to go ahead smoothly, joyfully, *and* simply?

Simple Pleasures

* Paint or refinish an old table. You might just make it a centerpiece for your home.
* Visit a home improvement store and gather some ideas for easy projects you could do.
* Take a class at one of these stores. Enjoy gaining knowledge and working toward a goal.

Wisdom for Living

Lord, I pray You would open my eyes to things that can add beauty and blessing to my home.

Hitting the Target

So we make it our goal to please him, whether we are at home in the body or away from it.

2 CORINTHIANS 5:9

If you don't have a target to shoot at, you'll never know if you have a hit or a miss! It is such a simple idea, but sometimes the simple ideas are the easy ones to overlook.

Goal setting doesn't just happen. We all have to take time to think long-range if we're going to have an effective plan. Those ten-year goals have to be made into smaller goals so that tomorrow you know how to proceed. Besides, when you are a mom, a ten-year plan is a bit of wishful thinking. Things change, your family's needs change. It is best to focus on short-term goals for this exercise.

We can fill our time with activities; that's easy. But goal setting directs us toward a purpose. If my goal for this summer is to read five books, then what book will I read first? If I want to memorize more Scripture, where will I begin tomorrow? Our goals become road maps for our life that constantly lead us around the next corner. That is the flow of life. You don't want to be so entrenched with goals that you miss the chances God gives you for healthy changes or even new goals. Keep it manageable so that your map works with the life you have. But also keep your eye on your destination. You will manage your time better, and you will have a sense of accomplishment when you reach the end of your journey toward a clearly defined goal.

Simple Pleasures

- Allocate ten minutes in the morning and ten in the evening for prayer.
- Plan a living room picnic for your children.
- Listen to music while you clean. Productive time can also be enjoyable time!

Wisdom for Living

*I want to keep my eye on You, Lord,
and work toward goals that are pleasing to You.*

Your Daily Planner

Those who plan what is good find love and faithfulness.

PROVERBS 14:22

A daily planner is a fantastic tool! "Uh-oh," you might say, "she's talking about planning and organizing again." Well, this is one tool we must discuss because it has made my life so much better. Honestly!

My daily planner almost never leaves my side. I keep an even larger version at home. My home instruction page is a weekly routine of chores and errands. A quick glance is all I need. Another section is for important numbers—everything from ambulance to veterinarian. Credit cards are listed in another section. You get the idea. One last tip. The larger notebook isn't always convenient, so I keep a daily reminder pad in my kitchen. Three columns on bright yellow paper: "Call," "do," and "see." Just take an hour or so to invest in your daily planner. It'll remove a major cause of stress in your life...disorganization. And you're on the way to a much more organized you!

A great benefit of this planner is you can schedule-in personal time and learn to stick with it. After all, just because you plan out your days does not mean that quiet moments cannot be a part of that. Idle time is not hurting you—wasted time is. Life is too precious to spend it frivolously or without purpose.

Simple Pleasures

- Present a time and money game plan to your family. Make it a fun day.
- Serve hot dogs and soda to set the mood of a ballpark or stadium meal.
- Assign team numbers and invent a cheer for motivation.

Wisdom for Living

Every day of my life matters! I want each one to count and be significant. Let me seek ways to get the most out of every moment You give me, Lord.

Something Borrowed

> *Give to the one who asks you, and do not turn away from the one who wants to borrow from you.*
>
> MATTHEW 5:42

Keeping track is a part of "keeping it simple." How many times have you tried to remember whom you loaned that card table to? Or that serving tray, cookbook, or pitcher? I was in the same boat until I misplaced some valuable items. To this day I haven't gotten them back. Oh, I'm sure they're being used by wonderful, friendly people who can't remember where they borrowed them from; nevertheless, each time I head to the hall closet to retrieve one of those items, I remember they are now part of that missing-in-action black hole.

The flip side of this situation is also important. I have often borrowed some household item or a friend's latest favorite book and completely forgotten to return it to them. So I designed a form to help me keep track of items I loan or borrow. It only takes a few seconds to jot down the details in a notebook. I list the date, the loaner/borrower's name, and any details about when they need it back. Try it.

Remember, it takes 21 days to learn a new habit. This habit will save you a lot of valuable time for the more important things in life!

Simple Pleasures

- Borrow your friend's children to give her some time for projects. Trade off!
- Borrow a great book from the library or a friend. Try one that is a little different from the books you usually read.
- Borrow a great line from a poem or a favorite Scripture. Memorize it!

Wisdom for Living

*Lord, help me to be aware of the blessings of time
and belongings You bring into my life,
and teach me to be a good steward of them.*

Sources and Resources

Come on, let's get organized! I know you've asked yourself, "What's the name of that florist who did such a great job for Sally's birthday?" Or "Where is that restaurant with the great kids' menu?" We often spend unnecessary time and energy flipping through the Yellow Pages or looking through a pile of notes in that messy drawer by the phone (mission impossible). Eliminate the problem by grouping phone numbers into categories such as bakeries, counselors, doctors, florists, whatever. Create a form called "Sources and Resources" and put it in a notebook. Being organized will save you a ton of time and frustration.

I will let you in on a little secret. A side benefit to easily accessible information is that others in the household can look up a phone number or address too. Just imagine that! Your kids, your husband, the baby-sitter...everyone can locate the resources that make life simpler. While all these people might think you are a walking, talking Rolodex, this list might cut down on the times they actually ask you to be their human phonebook.

If you give yourself 15 minutes a day to spend on better organization, you will enjoy the benefits it gives you and your family.

Simple Pleasures

* Organize a day off for yourself. Arrange for a baby-sitter and a clear schedule.
* Coordinate a child's birthday party with a local event—a parade, circus, or fair.
* Toss coupons of products you don't use. Don't be tempted to buy what you don't want.

Wisdom for Living

*Lord, may I value each and every moment of my day,
just as You value every precious moment of my life.*

Therefore, prepare your minds for action; be self-controlled; set your hope fully on the grace to be given you when Jesus Christ is revealed.

1 PETER 1:13

Money, money. Oh, how it can cause us grief when we let it control us instead of the other way around! I know, easier said than done. But one way to put money in its proper place is to use it wisely. How much money are you wasting at the supermarket? Did you know that after 30 minutes in the grocery store you'll spend 75 cents for every minute you stay there? The trick is to make up your shopping list and select the items you'll need before you go into the store.

Preplanning saves frustration and money. I guarantee you, it will help you become disciplined to only buy what's on the list. You can save anywhere from 15 to 20 dollars or more by sticking to that list. And, if possible, don't take the children with you when you shop. TV commercials influence what children want. It's unbelievable! They want stuff you've never even heard of. And it can be so easy to buy them a simple this or that to appease them. These little items add up quickly.

This plan has the added bonus of saving time. Instead of wandering the aisles while you try to remember that last item, you will have a strategy. No detours. Power shopping will get you home sooner and with more money in your purse.

Simple Pleasures

- Have a bowl of cereal for lunch and watch a television show.
- Spend time on the floor playing with your youngest child.
- Plant seeds for a great spring showing.

Wisdom for Living

Lord, help my focus be on the needs of my family.
May I avoid the list of silly wants or temptations
and keep my eye on ways to provide for my family
so that they are healthy and content.

Is Storage a Problem?

> In my Father's house are many rooms; if it were not so, I would have told you. I am going there to prepare a place for you.
>
> JOHN 14:2

Clutter and stuff. Where do you put it all? Does it sometimes seem as though clutter fills your spirit too? Simplify your surroundings and you will reap the reward of a more peaceful home and soul.

One idea is to cover some cardboard boxes with fabric. Add some trim and use them in any room of your house. Store rolled-up towels in a garage-sale wine rack or a wire bike basket attached to the wall. Hang Peg-Board in your kitchen for utensils and pots. Or how about this: Paint or stain a child's unfinished toy box and use it as a lamp table with lots of storage. Refinish an old chest of drawers to hold DVDs or CDs. If you're a basket collector, hang your baskets on one wall and use them to hold your napkins and table linens.

As you look for opportunities to use unique items for storage, don't forget to gather items you can throw away, give away, or sell at a garage sale. Removing clutter helps you organize those items that are the most important for you and your family. When everyday stuff has assigned places, you will discover you will feel more comfortable in your home.

Simple Pleasures

- Be prepared—keep a small box in the trunk with the following items: a first aid kit, a warm blanket, a quart of oil, windshield washer fluid, and a can of air for flat tires.
- Keep a small sewing kit in your purse for quick repairs.
- When your children have outgrown their cribs, car seats, and playpens, donate these items to your local women's shelter.

Wisdom for Living

Lord, thank You for the everyday items I have that make life easier.
Help me to take care of all my family's belongings
and create a place where rest and restoration abound.

Make Mealtimes Fun

Serve the LORD with fear and rejoice with trembling.

PSALM 2:11

When you think of a feast, what comes to mind? An elegant wedding reception? Thanksgiving dinner spread on a long, mahogany table? A rustic, outdoor barbeque with supper turning on the spit? Well, I have a surprise for you. A feast does not have to be a large-scale meal with elaborate party favors. I'd like to share with you how an everyday meal can become a small celebration.

First, it goes without saying that we turn off the television for mealtime. Mealtime is a time for sharing, but also for peace—a moment in the day when we celebrate togetherness. Oh, I know—it's not always easy. If you have a busy, active family, just getting everybody to eat at the same time is a chore. But it's worth the effort for at least one meal a day. It's worth taking the time and preparing the food—even if it's macaroni and cheese or take-out pizza. Turn off the noise, turn on the soft music, and light the candles. Create a feast for your family's eyes with a simple centerpiece or maybe use your good china for this mid-week dinner.

And as you take in the specialness of this meal, thank the Lord for blessing your time together. Then, simply celebrate your family!

Simple Pleasures

* Look for fun, interesting centerpieces to generate conversation at the table.
* Light a candle before a meal to set a soothing tone.
* Choose healthy foods so that your family is nourished.

Wisdom for Living

Father, help my family come together in celebration of our unity. Let our mealtimes become feasts of faith and love.

Eye-Catchers

The LORD will do what is good in his sight.

2 SAMUEL 10:12

Let the most obvious eye-catchers in any room of your home be beautiful and not merely utilitarian. You see not the ironing board, but the rose! I have some fantastic ideas to share with you on how to transform a work area into a beauty mark for your home.

Baskets, baskets, baskets! They're an inexpensive and attractive way to solve your work-area storage problems. If you don't have a desk, fill a cardboard box with office supplies and a lap desk and then store it in a closet or under a bed. Bookcases can hold more than books. Have you considered bookshelves for children's toys, sewing equipment, or office supplies? There are lots of clever and chic magazine racks available; use them to organize periodicals and other reading material. Use coffee mugs or colorful vases for pencils, pens, and paintbrushes.

File cabinets don't have to be ugly. Paint them to match your rooms. Or drape table runners over the top. Try decorating their tops with items you would otherwise store. Stack quilts or blankets under a lamp table, or hang them on a stair rail. The idea is to be organized and efficient without looking like a government office building!

Simple Pleasures

* Paint or refinish an old wood file cabinet to work with your décor.
* Create an office in a closet with shelves, cupboards, and storage drawers.
* Find or make a fabric screen to separate a corner work space from the rest of the room.

Wisdom for Living

Organize my days according to Your will, Lord.
Help me use my time to serve You and my family. Let me organize
my spiritual clutter and come to You as a clean, open vessel.

The Power of the List

Look to the LORD and his strength;
seek his face always.

1 CHRONICLES 16:11

Practice saying this, "I've got a list and I'm stickin' to it." Before you go to the grocery store, be sure you have this handy rule down pat. By adhering to an advance list you will get in and out of the market quickly, and you'll save yourself a lot of money in the long run. Having a list creates a shopping plan of action. This is very handy when you have the kids with you. If the item they want is one that was already discussed and officially put on the list, then it goes in the cart. Anything else of interest can be suggested for the next week's list. Of course, you have to abide by the rule too!

And definitely shop either early in the morning or late at night. Avoid the peak hours. Are you hungry? Then don't do any grocery shopping! You'll end up with a lot of stuff that you didn't need and probably shouldn't have. Buy your snack foods in bulk—they're cheaper. You can divide them up later with sealable plastic bags.

If you're buying clothes, take along a friend who's positive. If you're shopping in a store or mall with a huge parking lot, tie a ribbon on your antenna so you don't spend 15 embarrassing minutes looking for your car. See, shopping can really be hassle free.

Simple Pleasures

* Weed the garden. It is truly a refreshing way to spend an afternoon.
* Prepare a garden area for your children. Give them each an area to do what they wish.
* Do your shopping alone whenever possible. It will actually be a relaxing experience!

Wisdom for Living

I see Your goodness all around me, Lord. Let me be hungry
for what You offer me. Your provision takes care of my every need.

One Thing at a Time

The end of a matter is better than its beginning, and patience is better than pride.

ECCLESIASTES 7:8

Are you interested in adding just a little something that will brighten a bit of your home? You might actually have a list of things you would like to do...someday. But how about choosing one project for an upcoming weekend? Keep it really easy and manageable so you can finish it, and so you will be eager to try another weekender project next month. What will you choose? The possibilities are endless.

I was just reading that "tiles" are showing up everywhere around the home. With a little adhesive, grout, and a few tools you're all set for a whole new look! And I love greenery at the front door. You can get beautiful terra cotta pots—in fact, you probably have some in your garage right now. Use them for a grouping at the door. In times past, door knockers were a way to let people know the profession of the person in the house. Check out a flea market or buy one at the hardware store. Don't forget to make sure it's tarnish proof.

Just remember to keep things simple and stay within the time and money budget you have decided on. Come Monday, you will be so pleased with what your weekend project accomplished.

Simple Pleasures

- When you get stuck on a project, just imagine how great it will be when it is done.
- Complete something today. Finishing even a small task will encourage you.
- Help someone else finish a project that is long overdue.

Wisdom for Living

Thank You for creating me as a work in progress, Lord.
Piece by piece I work on my home. And bit by bit I work on
my spiritual life through prayer, fellowship,
and focused time in Your Word.

But I Don't Have Space

Where were you when I laid the earth's foundation? Tell me, if you understand.

JOB 38:4

I need more space! How often have you thought that? I want to share some ideas for one of the most common home-management problems: making space.

Here are some tips that can really help. Try installing a towel rack on the inside of the linen closet to hang tablecloths. You can use storage boxes. Stack them and put a round piece of plywood on top, and then cover it all with a pretty cloth. Who will know? Use the tops of cabinets, hutches, and refrigerators to store floral arrangements or baskets. Build a window seat under deep-set windows and use the space for storage. Seldom-used luggage is great for out-of-season clothing. The suitcases take up space anyway, so why not?

Let us not forget about cleaning out the closets and cupboards and drawers. Could someone else be using that ski jacket you haven't worn in five years? Those sweet baby clothes that evoke tender memories could be a part of another new mom's memories. Save out a few special pieces and give away the rest. You get space and help others.

God has more important things for you to do than juggle junk from place to place. Get organized and get focused on what matters to the Creator of the earth's foundation.

Simple Pleasures

- Take a bike ride alone or with the family. Enjoy your area's beauty.
- Journey out to a nearby farmer's market and buy fresh produce this weekend.
- Do you play an instrument? Pick it up again and enjoy the familiarity of making music.

Wisdom for Living

*Sometimes I think that if I move these boxes around one more time,
I will scream. Help me get organized, Lord.
I cannot wait to see how You will use me and my time.*

Ugh! Closets!

Who may ascend the hill of the LORD? Who may stand in his holy place? He who has clean hands and a pure heart, who does not lift up his soul to an idol or swear by what is false.

PSALM 24:3-4

Children's closets! Now there's a project for you. Wait! Don't put this book down until you hear me out. There are some tremendous benefits to tackling this task. I will help you, and you will be surprised to see how fun this can be. Let's get to work.

Keep everyday clothing items in their own colorful plastic bins on reachable shelves. You can also get color-coordinated child-size hangers. Use a lot of hooks inside the closets so the children can hang robes or coats. Build a shelf to run across the back or side of the closet to keep shoes organized. And by all means, compliment your children when they keep their clothing picked up.

Cleaning can become a lesson in giving as well. Gather the toys, clothing, and other items your child can give to others. Or have a toy-exchange party with neighborhood children. Your child will get the idea, and soon he or she will start loving the chance to give to others.

The idea isn't just to be neat—it's to teach responsibility. It's an opportunity for your child to really feel like a part of the family!

Simple Pleasures

- Turn up the music and dance barefoot with your children!
- Wear a wild hat while you clean house. You will laugh when you see your reflection.
- If you don't have a patio, create a space outdoors to enjoy as your own.

Wisdom for Living

*I want to raise a child who knows how to be responsible
and who finds joy in giving and growing.
Let me model this for my child, Lord.*

Where Did All the Money Go?

Do not conform any longer to the pattern of this world, but be transformed by the renewing of your mind.

ROMANS 12:2

Good money management is important because God associates our ability to handle spiritual matters with the ability to handle money. Did you know that? Luke 16:11 says: "If you're untrustworthy about worldly wealth, who will trust you with the true riches of heaven?" (NLT). Good question!

Check out these four characteristics of financial freedom: 1) your assets exceed your liabilities, 2) you're able to pay bills as they're due, 3) you have no unpaid bills, and 4) you're content with where you are. Bob and I have a saying: "If we aren't content with what we have, we'll never be content with what we want!" Money does not solve problems, but managing money can. If you live within the blessings you have, God will help you be content. Pray for wisdom, for joy in your circumstances, and for God to show you how to use your money to best serve Him.

Don't waste time on a wish list of things. Rather, place your focus on a list of heavenly riches. Ask God to show you how to increase your family time, your circle of friends, and your personal devotional time. You see? Non-money riches abound.

Money management is a lot about attitude! And contentment is right up there at the top of that heavenly riches list.

Simple Pleasures

- Make that list of heavenly riches while enjoying the sunset tonight.
- Experience the beauty of the world. Go on a walk by moonlight.
- Let your kids explore space through a telescope. Study God's vastness.

Wisdom for Living

Lord, my riches overflow. You have given me a heart that is extravagant with love and a spirit that is wealthy with Your grace.
Thank You for Your abundant provision of all I truly need.

May

CELEBRATING MOTHERHOOD

Children in the Kitchen

You still the hunger of those you cherish.

PSALM 17:14

Kitchens are wonderful places for children! You have probably had to shoo your little ones out of the kitchen more than once. Now I want you to consider ways to include your children in one of the best rooms in the house.

If you're a stay-at-home mom, as often as you can have some kind of delicious aroma coming from the oven or the stove when your children come home from school. It draws them in so wonderfully! On the weekend, let the children choose a recipe they would like to try. Assist them while giving them room to follow the instructions, figure out measurements, and see a list of ingredients turn into a tasty treat.

Children need to learn kitchen skills. Yes, even in this day and age! It'll be messy, but children are washable—and so is your kitchen. I consider that extra clean-up time a worthwhile investment in a future of happy kitchen hours—for myself and the next generation! I can't tell you what a thrill it is to visit my children now as adults, and I love it when they invite *me* into their grown-up kitchens!

Simple Pleasures

- Plant some herbs in little pots on your windowsill.
- Wear your hair differently today.
- Buy a new set of dish towels to add new colors to your kitchen.

Wisdom for Living

Father, when I teach my children how to cook, I am giving them room to make mistakes. I am letting them explore the riches of the kitchen, and I am giving them ingredients for life. Thank You for all You teach me.

Saving Time

> But I pray to you, O LORD, in the
> time of your favor; in your great
> love, O God, answer me with
> your sure salvation.
>
> PSALM 69:13

Keeping life simple in every area, even in meal preparation, is important and worth setting as a goal. Do you make meals much more difficult than they need to be?

At one point, I discovered I'd become a short-order cook! At breakfast it might be French toast for one, eggs for another, and cold cereal for someone else. I was pooped—and a bit put upon, I might add. The solution? To plan a week's worth of breakfasts, including each family member's favorites, one morning each week. Before you say, "Oh Emilie, get a life," hear me out! It became a *pleasure* to fix breakfast. The point is, if you don't enjoy the chores you have to do, how in the world is your family going to feel loved and cared for? And the other side of that coin is that by simplifying the task at hand, you are making life better for yourself. You have removed the element of stress or frustration from the situation and suddenly a chore becomes a blessing.

Having a good attitude while serving and caring for your family is important. Your children will reap the benefits when you simplify life so that you can become the woman God wants you to be.

Simple Pleasures

- Pray before preparing a meal. It will change how you feel about the task.
- Have iced tea or water with lemon to sip on while you fix a meal.
- Chop up a small plate of vegetables for you and eager children to nibble on before dinner.

Wisdom for Living

Dear Lord, help me to provide service with a smile!
I will seek to serve my family with a happy heart and face.
I will seek Your heart as I find ways to make life
better for the ones I love.

Saturday Chore Basket

The plans of the LORD stand firm forever, the purposes of his heart through all generations.

PSALM 33:11

Have you ever said "You mess up—you clean up!" to your children? Did it work? I have some tips on how to teach family responsibility. The end result is hopefully a more managed life and home so that you have time for other things.

There's no reason why mom has to pick up after everyone in the home. (Ah, I hear the distant sound of cheering!) Write on slips of paper all the tasks that need to be done each week. Put them in a basket, and every Saturday each of you pull out one or more for the coming week. Put a list of all the chores on your refrigerator and who is in charge that week. And that includes mom and dad. Everyone gets to help meet the responsibilities of the family.

Throughout these devotional times, we have discussed different ways to making life at home a little more manageable. Assigning chores and making them more enjoyable really comes down to teaching children about common courtesy, respect, and responsibility. When one of your children goes to someone else's home, is he or she the one who helps clean up or who offers to help? Breathing God's spirit of kindness and servanthood into your children will help build their godly character.

Simple Pleasures

- Invest in kindness. Be the one to go the extra mile in every situation today.
- Spend time in prayer asking for strength to be the mom God wants you to be.
- Write a note to your spouse encouraging him in his role as a parent.

Wisdom for Living

*Guide me, Lord, as I teach my children Your ways.
Help me to model those ways so that they understand
You are my source of strength and goodness.*

Work Space Face-Lifts

The eyes of all look to you, and you give them their food at the proper time. You open your hand and satisfy the desires of every living thing.

PSALM 145:15-16

Objects like file cabinets, refrigerators, and cabinetry can be decorated. Often these are the biggest eyesores in a room. And the most expensive elements to change...if you had to replace them, that is. But there are things you can do to create a new look without buying new pieces. The good news is you don't have to be stuck with the look you started with.

It is possible to have appliances professionally painted with great success. Kitchen cabinets can also get a face-lift with a coat of paint. Or remove the cabinet doors entirely and replace them with glass-paneled doors. Now that's a new look! Paint and paper the cabinet interior and line the shelf edges with lace. Or just try replacing the handles. What a difference even that can make!

Try changing the window treatments in a specific area. It is amazing how a different color can alter the feel of a room. People will wonder what is making the room so fresh. Put in a high shelf on a wall and place a vine plant so that it drapes and adds a nice visual to a boring wall.

If you want a simple golden rule for your house, here it is: "Have nothing in your house that you do not know to be useful or believe to be beautiful!"

Simple Pleasures

- Buy or make two new pillow coverings and add them to your living room.
- Visit a paint store and look at the beautiful colors. You might get some great ideas.
- Add a colored glaze to a plain wall for a lighter color transformation.

Wisdom for Living

Transformation is what faith is all about.
Lead me to a life that is transformed, Lord.
My heart and soul are born again in You.

A Tea Potluck

Did not the same one form us both within our mothers?

JOB 31:15

Our friends are the continuous threads that help hold our lives together. I have a wonderful way for you to nurture a group of friends— a "Tea Potluck." It's quite simple and the perfect party for a circle of women. With a little planning and care, you can bring a sense of intimacy to a much larger group than two or three. It's especially great for hosting a planning meeting, for the women in your church, or for coworkers. Plus, it's a great way to widen your circle of friends and have a wonderful time in the process. The fun of a "potluck" is to enjoy sampling the goodies and enjoying the fellowship of others. Have everyone bring a snack to share that will go well with tea. Provide the tea, or if you are inviting a few tea enthusiasts, have them bring their favorite kind. If you are introducing a few people to the pleasures of tea, include a little welcome package with a recipe for tea along with a teatime blessing.

Once you do this, you will likely want to do it again. It is a soothing way to spend time with friends or coworkers. Much can get done over a pot of tea. And it won't feel like work at all.

This get-together may require an extra bit of planning—and a tip or two from one of the many tea books available—but feel free to use your creativity and go for it!

Simple Pleasures

- Make a reservation at a local tea shop. Invite a friend for a nice quiet talk.
- Ask relatives, especially older ones, if they remember any tea traditions in your family. Record them to share with your children later.
- Sip a cup of tea as you think of friends that are especially close to you. Ask God to bless their day.

Wisdom for Living

May I always be a good friend to others.
Lord, show me how to give and receive friendship.

Friends Forever

I will declare that your love stands firm forever, that you established your faithfulness in heaven itself.

PSALM 89:2

What is there about a good friend that makes her so special? Sometimes the simple answer is the most profound: You like her! You feel better when she's around. When was the last time you took a moment to send your friend a little note...a surprise in an otherwise crazy day? Pick something that really stands out—put your note in a red envelope with a few stickers here and there. Maybe even include an invitation to tea or a gift certificate at one of the local coffee shops. Or if you really want to make a statement, tuck in a certificate for a "spa day" so that just the two of you can have the time of your life!

You can create a spa day at your own home too. If you and your friend both have children who are at school during the day, spend a couple hours one day soaking your feet in the tub and then enjoying a face mask while watching an old, romantic comedy. Such a simple thing can be just what you and your friend need.

Send your friend a quick postcard now and then just to say hi. Tell her one thing you really enjoy about your time with her. Let her know she is special and loved. Send her a Scripture verse as a reminder that God loves her.

Taking time for friendships will add great joy to your life.

Simple Pleasures

* Invite some close friends for a simple dinner to catch up on each other's lives.
* Invite a friend's children over for the afternoon. Make popcorn and watch movies.
* Surprise a faraway friend with a phone call. Hearing your voice will brighten her day.

Wisdom for Living

What a friend we have in Jesus. That is what the old hymn says, Lord. You are my best friend. You know my heart as I seek Yours.

You're Stylin'

You turned my wailing into dancing; you removed my sackcloth and clothed me with joy, that my heart may sing to you and not be silent. O LORD my God, I will give you thanks forever.

PSALM 30:11-12

What does style have to do with anything? Believe me, when it comes to decorating, style matters. Let me be more specific...*your* style matters. I gave up a long time ago trying to impress people with my decorating style. Better to just be myself and people can have their own preferences! So trust yourself...your most creative, expressive, beautiful self.

Creating a lovely home is simply a matter of taking your tastes, your personality, and your possessions and showing them with their best face on. What are the things you love? The activities you enjoy? What brings you pleasure? What colors do you like? Do you like wide-open spaces or small nooks and crannies for private retreats? Are you fond of big floral prints or bold single colors against each other?

You may not even know how to define your style to others. And that is okay. Why do we love certain houses—and why do they seem to love us? It's the warmth of our individual hearts that we reflect in our surroundings. You're going to do fine. You've pretty much got that style thing goin'.

Simple Pleasures

* Sit on your couch and think about what it is that reflects your personal style in the room.
* Move a piece of furniture from one room to another. You might discover a new use for it.
* Pretend you are an interior decorator hired for your own home. What would you tell you?

Wisdom for Living

*God, You gave me a style all my own. I won't try to fit it into someone else's definition of beautiful or tasteful.
I want to love my home and create a place
that celebrates my family's unique personality.*

A Family Legacy

I will sing of the LORD's great love forever; with my mouth I will make your faithfulness known through all generations.

PSALM 89:1

Why not take a day and dig through storage boxes, flip through photo albums, and discover again things that bring you joy? I don't know about you, but I enjoy the simple things of life!

A delicate cut-glass vase, a child's drawing, a grandfather's old letters. For me it's worthwhile when it brings to mind my most loved relationships, my dearest memories. That old family Bible with the pictures of relatives that make you chuckle—and who you hope you don't end up looking like! These are some of the things that make up your heritage. Enjoy them.

Think of other family stories...those in the Bible that tell of your Christian faith lineage. That too is a heritage to hold dear, to learn from, and to pass along to your children just as you would tell them stories about your parents and grandparents.

In all that you do for your children, give them a sense of the past and the anticipation of their future as a member of your family—and as a member of God's family! This is a gift that will stay with them forever.

Simple Pleasures

* Take your children to a park and play a game from your childhood.
* Listen to an old record or recording of music you grew up with.
* Before bed, say the "Now I lay me down" prayer with the faith of a child.

Wisdom for Living

Father, when I tell stories, I connect my children to their family and to You. They are given as examples of Your faithfulness to each generation.

An Old Rolling Pin

He settles the barren woman in her home as a happy mother of children.

PSALM 113:9

Can you believe that today I am going to tell you a story about an old rolling pin? My friend Donna's grandmother was raised in an orphanage until she was 13. She married an immigrant, a widower with one small son. The only thing she brought to her marriage was a merry laugh, the ability to care for a home, and her talent for cooking! When grandpa died and grandma came to live with Donna's family, the only thing she brought with her was an old rolling pin. It had seen a lot of years of loving service. Even the worn handles were beautiful to Donna. They represented endless cakes and pies and other wonderful-smelling goodies. This rolling pin became one of Donna's "timeless treasures" that she passed along to her daughter. Just a plain old rolling pin? Not on your life. It's an important part of a family legacy.

Why do I share such a story? I want to remind you of the everyday treasures you use, including heirlooms, household items, and—most of all—words! Everyday words of blessing, thankfulness, and encouragement will shine brightly in your child's heart, and they will pass this gift of kindness along to their children. Just a plain old expression of love? Not on your life. It's an important part of a family legacy.

Simple Pleasures

- Learn to say "I love you" in three languages. Surprise your spouse.
- Move a chair to face a window with a view and enjoy your tea from a new perspective.
- Go to the library and spend an hour reading in a quiet corner.

Wisdom for Living

Dear Lord, I want to raise my children surrounded by treasures of loving words. May my faith in You never be a buried treasure, but one exposed, shared, and celebrated in my family's history.

As a mother comforts her child, so will I comfort you.

ISAIAH 66:13

Have you tried more than a few times to motivate your child to clean his or her room? How has that worked for you? I thought so. Over the years I have learned that children are a lot like adults when it comes to areas of responsibility. If they are involved in the initial decisions on some level, they will feel more responsible for the end result.

I believe a person who has to occupy a room should have a say in how it looks. The more input a child has, the more likely he or she will care about keeping it clean. Well, we can hope, can't we? My granddaughter stenciled the names of her friends in several colors on one wall of her room. The other walls were painted in stripes of the same colors, with linens and drapes picking up the theme. We loved it when we saw it! Provide a space that encourages children to draw, paint, build, act, create. It's also a great time in their little lives to encourage a place and a time for learning God's Word and for praying with them.

Developing this kind of pride of ownership and sense of responsibility in a child is wonderful. You might even see a child more willing to tackle other projects or chores when they can apply their own style to how they are done.

Simple Pleasures

* Make a game out of cleaning. Have each item your children put away be worth points.
* Take before and after pictures of a child's room to motivate them.
* Offer the reward of a picnic in their room if they finish cleaning by dinnertime.

Wisdom for Living

Lord, help me train my child in Your ways. I want to make room for each child's personality and creativity in our home.

Share Your Life in Pictures

May your father and mother be glad; may she who gave you birth rejoice!

PROVERBS 23:25

Collections of any kind are usually a way for people to share stories. Do you collect teacups or spoons or stuffed animals? If so, I'll bet you can share with any visitor where you got each and every one or who gave you this one as a birthday gift four years ago.

But have you ever thought of your family photos as a collection? By gathering together these special treasures and displaying them in fun ways, you can brighten your home with the faces you love!

One of my tables has photos of the women in my family. They cover several generations. Though I display them in a variety of frames, it's the mother-daughter-granddaughter motif that pulls the collection together. And it gives me a great opportunity to share the lives and hearts of the people in the pictures. You can group black-and-white photos in a group. Another idea is to change the pictures with the seasons. Whenever you display any collection or group items together, remember to stage a surprise! Make sure there's one element that's a little quirky—just by being different. Collections are just another way of sharing yourself with others.

Simple Pleasures

- Gather wedding photos from other family members and generations. Create an album.
- Photograph spiritual growth moments like baptisms, church camp, and Sunday school.
- Have children draw pictures of their memories. Frame these alongside photos.

Wisdom for Living

Dear God, as I gather together the images of my loved ones, may I be reminded to pray for these special people in my life.

Lessons from a Teacup

Can a mother forget the baby at her breast and have no compassion on the child she has borne?

ISAIAH 49:15

The lessons a mother passes on to her child is part of that child's heritage. And often these guidelines for life revolve around the simplest of concepts. My mother taught me the practical skills of running a home—preparing meals, washing clothes. She also passed along her knack for sewing and her love of fine fabrics, and later in her life, the basics of business as I worked beside her in the dress shop. Are you thinking of what your mother taught you? Are they lessons you are passing along to your own child?

I learned other lessons as well. Some were less tangible but just as important. In fact, more important. Mama showed me that you keep going when life gets hard and that you don't have to wait until things are perfect before inviting others into your life. When life is difficult, it is important to see whom God might be sending your way to provide comfort, encouragement, and even guidance.

I learned from her that you can easily turn a kettle of hot water and a couple of cups of tea into a full-blown celebration! From our little tea parties I learned how important it is to give ourselves to others and be filled with the love poured into us by them.

Simple Pleasures

- Tea travels! Take some tea pouches over to a friend's house for a pleasant tea break.
- Let your child enjoy tea, punch, or water from a teacup. It will make them feel special.
- Tea is for boys too! Teach young boys gentlemanly table manners with a teatime.

Wisdom for Living

It is sometimes difficult to ask for help or seek friendship when life is really hard. Lord, help me to be like an empty cup, waiting to receive the love of others.

Chores!

> What a lioness was your mother among the lions! She lay down among the young lions and reared her cubs.
>
> EZEKIEL 19:2

The word "chores" can send the children running out the back door. But if you approach chores in a clever way, these acts of labor will help your children feel they are part of the family. This might sound a bit old-fashioned, but it is true. So if you needed a good reason to stand firm on the enforcement of chores, you just heard it from me.

One young mother said to me, "Emilie, my kids have friends who've never had to help empty a dishwasher." I didn't want to tell her there's a whole generation of us who didn't even have dishwashers! That 12-year-old of yours could make dinner once a week—and your 8-year-old can certainly do the laundry. Okay, when the shock wears off, let me encourage you that your children need to do their share in your home. They might grumble or they might actually blossom under their contribution to the family. Much of their response will relate to how you present the chores. If the duties are fairly distributed and your children see how you and your husband cooperate to get your own chores done, this will all feel normal, comfortable, and worthwhile to a child.

If it sounds a bit countercultural—it is! But over the years I've discovered how important it is for your children to learn responsibility, and what better place than in your home?

Simple Pleasures

- Place hard candies throughout a room a child is cleaning so she will be extra thorough.
- Pray out loud with your young children. Teach them to talk to God openly.
- Always praise a child for honoring his commitments.

Wisdom for Living

My hard work is a model for my child's future work ethic.
Lord, help my attitude be positive and encouraging.
May serving others be seen as a privilege.

"I Love You" Assignments

Because your love is better than life, my lips will glorify you.

PSALM 63:3

How can you share the responsibility of preparing a big meal and keeping the guests happy and feeling welcome? I have a great idea for you to try. Create "I love you because" cards the next time you're the hostess for that big family dinner. Maybe it will even be Mother's Day or your birthday, and your home is still the main place people come together. Here is how it works for everyone: Write "I love you because you get to serve the dessert." "I love you because you get to mash the potatoes." And so on. Write enough cards for everyone who's coming and place them in a basket. Let each one draw from the "I love you" basket. Everyone will not only take their duties seriously—they will do them cheerfully. While you might think you are putting guests to work, you are really inviting them to be a part of the meal on every level. You are welcoming them to share in the preparation like family. Just think how awkward you have felt as a visitor to someone's home when you did not know how to be of assistance without feeling in the way. Now, nobody will be left out.

The day will breeze by with everyone chipping in and having a great time. And mom, you get a break! Later, go around the table and thank the Lord for each of your family and friends. Pretty simple!

Simple Pleasures

- When you visit friends for dinner, bring a small hostess gift for their children.
- Teach your children "I love you" in sign language.
- Sing "Jesus Loves Me" as a family.

Wisdom for Living

Father, as a member of the body of Christ, I am part of such a wonderful, extended family. Help me to always find ways to include these brothers and sisters in celebrations of life.

A Mother's Hands

She opens her arms to the poor and extends her hands to the needy.

PROVERBS 31:20

A mom has to be able to run on black coffee and leftovers. She has to have a kiss that can cure anything from a broken leg to a disappointing relationship. She has to have six pairs of hands and ears that can listen, hear, and interpret every need of her family.

You are one of those moms. Just think what an important part of God's creation you are—the glue that holds your family together. We need millions of mothers who understand their roles and proceed with great confidence. We need moms who will stand boldly before the world and not budge. Never feel ashamed of your commitment to such a vital job. And never second-guess that your role of mother is anything less than significant and God-pleasing!

We need you very much—don't give up the task God has given you. The world needs godly women who will model and promote righteousness. Create for yourself a network of other moms who share your convictions, who will inspire you to be your best, and who will encourage you during the hard days.

Call a mom who needs affirmation and tell her what a great job she's doing! And if that mom is *your* mom—so much the better!

Simple Pleasures

* Thank God for motherhood!
* Spend a morning remembering the birth of each child in your family.
* Be still and spend time in prayer. Lift up the needs you have as a mother to your Father.

Wisdom for Living

A mother's heart is close to You, God. May women seek Your help and Your strength as they commit to forming lives and establishing a foundation of faith for their children.

A Happy Heart

Delight yourself in the LORD and he will give you the desires of your heart.

PSALM 37:4

The Scriptures are quite clear that a thankful heart is a happy heart. When I'm appreciative for all I have, my mental, physical, and spiritual dimensions are in balance. The family chores run smoother and the entire mood of my home is more relaxed. I'm excited each day, challenged by what may come my way. People like to be around people who are positive and edifying. Choosing your words carefully relates to choosing a good attitude. Are you encouraging and uplifting? Or are you negative to yourself and to your family with harsh words or an irritated tone? Think of words that make you happy and use them frequently! Make it a game you play with yourself each day. Use a new happy word for the day. Maybe it will come from your morning Scripture reading. Try this, and you will experience the joy in this exercise!

We need to take our eyes off of stuff and become women of thanksgiving. When we're thankful, possessions are in proper perspective and we are so much happier! Take time tonight to let your family know how thankful you are for all that God has given you!

Simple Pleasures

- Have a warm cup of soup today with a cheese sandwich.
- Add lace to the edges of curtains for extra dimension.
- Watch an old musical comedy and sing along.

Wisdom for Living

I desire a heart of contentment and joy, Lord.
Help me dwell on Your Word and make its language
my vocabulary of happiness when I speak to my family.

The Ideal Woman

You are forgiving and good, O Lord, abounding in love to all who call to you.

PSALM 86:5

Being a Christian woman and mother today is not easy. There are many voices within our culture and society that diminish the value of being a woman of faith and a caretaker for your family. For years I struggled with the idea of worth in my work. I was a homemaker with five children. I was always tired, with little energy for anything else—including romancing my husband. I constantly struggled with self-worth. As you can suspect, I wasn't too exciting to be around! But something gave me new insight.

A woman shared Proverbs 31 with me, and it changed my life. I encourage you to explore this wonderful chapter of God's Word. It shows that the ideal Hebrew woman handled many activities outside the home, but she also remained focused on her husband, children, and household. What's in it for me as a woman? Proverbs 31:28 gives me my blessing: "Her children arise and call her blessed; her husband also, and he praises her." Without a doubt, I know God has confirmed the work of my hands.

Do you have days when you doubt the importance of your work? Listen to God's voice in the Scripture. Your life as a mother is a life of significance before the Lord.

Simple Pleasures

- Write a letter to your husband or to a friend by candlelight.
- Prepare fish with lemon and garlic and rosemary for a delicious supper.
- Use a blank book or journal and make a list of good books as you read them.

Wisdom for Living

My worth is established in Your eyes, Lord. I will not feel guilty or ashamed for choosing to live a righteous life as a woman of faith whose heart is focused on her family.

Dump the Supermom

Joshua told the people, "Consecrate yourselves, for tomorrow the LORD will do amazing things among you."

JOSHUA 3:5

Are you weary, my friend? Do you have days when you think you just cannot continue at the same pace, reach the same goals, meet all the needs of your family? I understand. What you do is not easy. Let me help you help yourself.

First of all, Supermom has to go. The image of the woman who does it all and does it without any help from her family has got to go. Get your family together and let them know you need their assistance. They'll come through for you. Make a list ahead of time of ways they can help out.

Second, communicate on a personal level with your family. Share your feelings concerning homework, friends, and especially about God.

Third, teach your children as you work side by side. When children bake cookies with me, or we make a salad, wash a car, whatever—we're a team. It's amazing what I found out about our children and their feelings as we worked together. I was there—available. In turn, they learned to work. I can't tell you how many times our conversations turned in spiritual directions. After all, isn't that what it's all about?

Simple Pleasures

- Ask for help when you need it.
- Look at the day ahead. Are you duplicating any trips, errands, or tasks? Consolidate!
- Make a bowl of popcorn mid-morning. Snack on that throughout the day.

Wisdom for Living

Dear Father, I don't want to miss out on any of the important stuff, so I hereby give up the title Supermom and willingly accept my role as Satisfied Mom. I will focus on what counts!

A Mom Card

> Those who know your name will
> trust in you, for you, LORD, have
> never forsaken those who seek
> you.
>
> PSALM 9:10

If you're a mom, you need a business card! Oh, I know, you're probably saying, "What? A business card?" My sister-in-law gave me some calling cards when our children were little. They had my name, telephone number, and then all around the card were the fun things that I like to do. I couldn't believe how much I used those cards. I'd see a mother at school who would tell me her son was going to come home with my son. Instead of fumbling through my purse finding a pen and piece of paper so I could give her my phone number, I'd zip out my business card. "That's neat," was always the reply. Followed by, "I didn't know you made homemade bread," or "I didn't know you taught a time management class."

If you work outside the home, personal calling cards can list a work number, home number, cell phone number, and e-mail address. When your child stays with a child-care provider, this card will contain all the information you want them to have on hand.

These cards are very inexpensive to make. Visit your local copy shop and check into this idea. If your phone number changes, you can toss the old cards, print a new batch, and send the updated version with your Christmas cards this year. Simple as can be.

Simple Pleasures

- Sketch out ideas for your card. Make an afternoon of it with a friend.
- Dream about what kind of business you would run if you could.
- Take your husband to lunch.

Wisdom for Living

*I have an important job, Lord. I pray for strength to be
a good mother and to be proud of this job title all of my life.*

Rejoice in Who You Are

> My dove, my perfect one, is unique, the only daughter of her mother, the favorite of the one who bore her.
>
> SONG OF SONGS 6:9

Being a woman with your own calling and purpose is such a privilege! Do you feel that way? If you are like most women, some days being a woman feels like a whole lot of work. Today, I want to encourage you in your God-given gift.

Women seem to have an innate ability to transform their surroundings—to make them comfortable and inviting. Frankly, I think we should rejoice in that! It doesn't mean we all have to be the same. When I think feminine, I think of soft colors, lace, and flowers. But other women I know wear their tailored or casual cotton clothes with a flair that is both feminine and creative. This spirit of femininity is so many things. To me, it is objects chosen for their beauty as well as their usefulness. It's lovingly caring for not only our beautiful things but, more importantly, our family. It's people nurtured and accepted. It's simply loveliness embraced and shared. And that comes in a whole lot of different packages. Wouldn't you agree?

As a woman of God, your expression of your creativity is your gift to yourself, to God, and to others. Your style makes a unique imprint in the world around you. Trust it!

Simple Pleasures

* Call a sister or brother and tell them hi.
* Bring nature indoors with lots of fresh flowers.
* If you have a porch, be sure you have at least a folding chair ready to go out there.

Wisdom for Living

When I feel myself hold back my style, Lord, may I turn the situation over to You. May I adorn myself with confidence in my Creator who loves me and made me special!

Tea...for You, for Them

*If you have any encouragement
from being united with Christ, if
any comfort from his love, if any
fellowship with the Spirit, if any
tenderness and compassion, then
make my joy complete by being
like-minded, having the same love,
being one in spirit and purpose.*

PHILIPPIANS 2:1-2

I don't know about you, but just say the word and I'm ready for tea! I think this is because taking time for tea is taking time to be centered, calm, reflective. It brings balance to a day that is crazy or a relationship that is out of sync.

My friend Sheri uses tea parties to stay close to her daughter. "We do tea parties all the time," she tells me. Every Christmas morning they get up and have a tea party before everybody else is up. They have tea parties on the first day of school—and anytime they're not connecting. Light a candle, arrange a centerpiece, and pull out something you've baked. Then have a wonderful time together. Share yourself along with the cookies and crumpets. Sweeten your teatimes with trust and affection. Use the occasion to say the things you may not have shared before, and let your daughter or your special friend know how much they mean to you!

Talk to God together too. Introduce to your child the joy of communicating with the Lord. Make it a natural part of her day, and it will stay with her forever.

Simple Pleasures

* Create a raised garden bed for your vegetables.
* Decide what your big yard project will be for the season ahead.
* Create a path with a few stepping stones and have it lead to a chair or bench.

Wisdom for Living

*Moments of calm conversation. Expressions of gratitude.
Delving into hurts or problems. This is how I want to communicate
with You, Lord. Let my child know You intimately too.*

June

BEAUTY AND THE BEST

Beautiful Results

Charm is deceptive, and beauty is fleeting; but a woman who fears the LORD is to be praised.

PROVERBS 31:30

Making beauty out of something ordinary will bring you a lot of joy! Just placing a single flower in a bud vase and setting it on a windowsill can transform a room. Your focus shifts from the peeling paint on the cupboard to this tiny, beautiful spot of color against the sunshine.

I love to watch a brightly colored afghan emerge from a basket of yarn. Or a beat-up old table do a Cinderella act under the magic wand of a paintbrush. Or the fun of serving brunch on matching pottery and linens. It's even more fun if I found the pottery at a garage sale! And you know what? Creativity doesn't have to be totally original. You can find ideas in magazines or through friends or even from our days together in this book.

And creativity isn't just for self-fulfillment. Much of the joy comes in sharing it with others. Share the act of creating. Include your children in a creative endeavor. Let them assist you in making decisions. You will be inspired by your child's imagination, and they will see that they have a lot to offer. So let's be bold when it comes to sharing our creativity! It's a wonderful way to showcase God's love and creativity in our lives.

Simple Pleasures

* Wear a color you don't usually wear. See how it feels for a day.
* Rinse your face with water and witch hazel for a refreshing beginning to the day.
* In the evening, soak your feet in the tub as you read your nightly devotions.

Wisdom for Living

You created the world in six days, Lord.
You created man out of dirt. I want Your creation to be
my inspiration. Colors, shapes, shadows, light…thank You.

A Sense of Smell

What's the first thing you do when you pick a rose? Me too. I hold it up close to my nose and I breathe in beauty. Isn't God glorious? Beauty can enter our lives through our sense of smell. Amazing.

A beautiful fragrance in a home can brighten everyone's day. Spray a little cologne on your notepaper or greeting cards. During holiday times, add the fragrance of the season to your life by boiling a little pot of cinnamon and other spices on the stove. Enjoy your other senses as well. Put on lively music while you do housework. Take time out with some praise music and your Bible. Experiment with herbs and spices in your cooking, and don't be afraid to try new dishes.

Let's embrace this statement with joy: There's nothing self-indulgent about such small pleasures! Allow that to sink in. When our lives are busy, we begin to think such endeavors are trivial and even ungodly. But just remember, these small joys are God's gifts, and we can be grateful to Him for them. It's amazing how these simple things can help you to regroup, prioritize, and pray! Cultivate them in your life simply and gratefully.

Simple Pleasures

- Plan a summer vacation for your family.
- Have the children prepare for the summer by boxing up last season's clothes.
- Schedule a garage sale soon to kick off the season and clean house.

Wisdom for Living

Lord, help me take the time to stop and smell the roses. And when I do, I will think of how You made us to enjoy the beauty of Your creation. I will take time to breathe in the fragrance of life.

Pluck, Color, Brush, and Cream

The King will greatly desire your beauty; because He is your Lord, worship Him.

PSALM 45:11 NKJV

Are you taking the trouble to make the best of what God has given you? I certainly hope so! I have a few thoughts on being a beautiful woman.

I'll never look like a model or a movie star, but I can honor God by taking care of the unique "me" He has created. That's one reason to be faithful to an exercise program. Those daily walks or workouts can help keep the figure under control—to say nothing about restoring energy. They also give me a sense of well-being and make it easier to reach out to others. Shiny hair, healthy nails, fresh skin all relate directly to the food you put in your body. Caring for yourself is not a silly matter, but a way to take care of the heart and soul God gave you. I think women can sometimes become so caught up in caring for others that their health and beauty are ignored. God doesn't want that. He wants you to be whole and happy.

So take the time to pluck, color, brush, and cream! You'll feel more beautiful, and your actions will tell the world you care about what God has created!

Simple Pleasures

- Drink water with lemon to get your day started.
- Look in the mirror and tell God something you like about what you see.
- Go to the mall and walk around for 30 minutes.

Wisdom for Living

I am a designer original. I will love the body and spirit I was given by You, Lord. And I will show it love by caring for my needs.

Ruffles and Perfume

Your beauty should not come from outward adornment...Instead, it should be that of your inner self, the unfading beauty of a gentle and quiet spirit, which is of great worth in God's sight.

1 PETER 3:3-4

We cannot let our discussion of beauty merely include physical attributes. True beauty is beyond our body, our skin, our hair. I believe in taking care of myself and my surroundings—I love beautiful things around me. But if I put all my energy into "self-care," I've missed the whole point.

True beauty comes from within. If that's lacking, no exercise program, eating plan, or wardrobe miracle can put it there! Ruffles or perfume are not a substitute for inner beauty. When we meet a truly charming and kind person, the first impression is usually that of beauty. You might not even recall their features later, but their genuine spirit touched you in a lovely way.

True beauty comes from the heart. That's why I need the message of 1 Peter 3 to remind me that beauty should be "that of your inner self, the unfading beauty of a gentle and quiet spirit, which is of great worth in God's sight." For this is the way the holy women of the past made themselves beautiful.

Simple Pleasures

- Open all the curtains and blinds today. Spend a day in the sunshine.
- Clean your baseboards and the top of shelves. Then take a break with a tall iced tea.
- Start a notebook to record your family tree.

Wisdom for Living

God, let me not only nurture the beauty within me, but may I also be one who seeks beauty in others. May I appreciate the wonder of the spirit You have created in them.

Time for an Update

How lovely is your dwelling place,
O LORD Almighty!

PSALM 84:1

Are you thinking it's time to update your home? Don't panic! There really are simple ways to do this. And you will have *fun* in the process. Plan to do this without spending any money. Make it a goal to add five new touches of warmth to your home using items that are already tucked away or in a corner going unnoticed.

Most of us have furniture or accessories of some kind, even if it's our "early married" stuff. It's a place to start. Look at what you have and see if it can't be "transformed" into something else! A stray cup and saucer can be filled with potpourri and perched on top of a stack of books next to an old pair of eyeglasses. Look at new ways to use tassels, hooks, drawer pulls, even costume jewelry. Bring out old linens or even heirloom pieces and find a way to show them off. You can still keep them protected in shadow boxes or frames while sharing their history and warmth with those in your home. Elements that tie your past and present surround your family with heritage.

Simple Pleasures

- Place daisies throughout the house to bring in a bit of sunshine.
- Light aromatic candles throughout the house to add a feeling of warmth.
- Repot some houseplants to give them an updated look.

Wisdom for Living

What can I discover today in my own home that will
add warmth to a room? What treasures are in my heart today,
Lord, that I can share with another?

Keep Dreaming

*The Spirit of God has made me;
the breath of the Almighty gives
me life.*

JOB 33:4

Don't let a tiny budget keep you from dreaming! Keep a notebook of decorating ideas you like. Then when you do have the money or the materials, you'll know what you want to do. And remember, handmade items like wall hangings, pillows, wood carvings, and dolls are wonderful for creating a warm, personal look. If you can't make things yourself, try craft sales or commission a friend to help you. And children's art is wonderful! Go ahead and frame those crayon drawings. Your family and guests will love them.

If you love perusing gardening and home-style magazines, tear out pages of designs, colors, and ideas you like. Add these to your notebook, organizing them according to room categories. Revisit them for fun and when you are ready to start on a project. Next time you stay in a charming hotel or in someone's home, take pictures of the elements that please you and create the atmosphere you want in your home. You are creating a photo album of dreams! Add them to the notebook too. Keep the inspiration alive.

Simple Pleasures

- Sit down with your children and have them draw a picture of their dream house.
- Talk with them about what they might want to be when they grow up.
- Ask them what their Creator might want them to be.

Wisdom for Living

*I want a home that is all about Your amazing grace,
Father. I will hold to this vision as I make plans
and create a sanctuary for myself and my family.*

Keep Your Promises

The LORD is faithful to all his promises and loving toward all he has made.

Just do what you say you are going to do. Not a bad piece of advice. I am not pointing a finger. I too have had to learn the importance of keeping promises and being honest with the people in my life. It is amazing how the little things can trip us up. We must stay focused on being honorable witnesses to the Lord's goodness.

"I got tied up and forgot." "I was just too tired." And so the excuses go. I suggest you don't make promises if you can't keep them. This has a lot to do with managing your time and priorities. It helps to determine your objectives and how you wish to invest in time for ministry and outreach and service. Then, when an offer comes up and time is short and the area is not in line with your gifts or your personal ministry focus, just say no.

When we keep our promises, we teach people we are trustworthy. You'll be amazed how many people will be pleasantly surprised when you honor your commitments. When you are careful about saying yes and do so willingly and with the intention of fulfilling the promise, you will be someone people can count on. And don't forget to seek advice from the One *you* can count on when you have to make decisions about time and priorities.

Simple Pleasures

- When in doubt, flip a coin. Take care of the other task tomorrow.
- Really think about what you want to commit your time to.
- Make a plan for how to make your yes a yes and your no a no.

Wisdom for Living

*God, You keep Your promises. I am so grateful that You do.
I desire to model this aspect of Your character in my life.
Help me to become more like You each day.*

The Flea Factor

One thing I ask of the LORD, this is what I seek: that I may dwell in the house of the LORD all the days of my life, to gaze upon the beauty of the LORD and to seek him in his temple.

PSALM 27:4

The "Flea Factor" can change the way you shop and decorate. That's right. Flea Factor. Garage sales, swap meets, flea markets, and estate sales are great sources for decorating magic! Just watch out for large-scale antique dealerships with inflated prices and often poor merchandise. But these stores can be great sources of unique accessories if you know what you like. Just stick to your budget. I know of a church in our area where the "rummage sale" each year is one of the hottest spots in town for that particular weekend. If you go on a weekend trip or a longer family vacation, check out the area you are visiting. It is great fun to see the different types of "finds" in other states or even areas of your home state. That set of plates you have been scouring your markets for...maybe it will be waiting for you in a small town just a day's drive away.

You wouldn't believe some of the incredible bargains and wonderful pieces that are available. Keep an eye out for estate sales and auctions. A few weekends of treasure hunting, a little creativity on your part, and you may locate just the piece you've needed for your beautiful home.

Take a close look at your surroundings, and gaze upon the beauty of the Lord's blessings in your life. Praise Him and thank Him today.

Simple Pleasures

- Add some old hand towels to your kitchen's motif.
- Hang lacey aprons on your wall for color and decoration.
- Drape an old television tray with a red-and-white checkered cloth and use it as a plant stand.

Wisdom for Living

Lord, I want to make a discovery today!
Let me find a hidden joy within my family and my life.

A Good Start

You will also be a crown of beauty in the hand of the LORD, and a royal diadem in the hand of your God.

ISAIAH 62:3 NASB

Take a little time to start the day right. It can make all the difference in your attitude and state of mind for the next 24 hours.

Here's a routine that helps me. Get out of bed and make the bed (unless your husband is still in it). Take a minute to stretch and touch your toes. Then shower, put a little "paint on the barn," and dress in whatever is best for that day. After that, find a favorite place and sit down with your coffee or tea in the quiet of the morning. Spend a little time with God before the hectic day really starts. Ask Him to help your heart beat with joy the whole day long. Ask to be aware of how you interact with your children, your husband, coworkers, and others. Offer up your day to God. This loving discipline will really change your daily perspective when faced with stressful times and happy moments.

Start the day with a positive attitude. Choose joy! You're a new person ready to meet the challenges of a new day. Simple, isn't it? The best things always are!

Simple Pleasures

* What gives you joy? Let your thoughts go to such things today while you do tasks.
* Be a giver of joy to your family. Plan a night of popcorn, games, or movies.
* Make your children laugh every day!

Wisdom for Living

O God, You are the Creator of sunshine, flowers, rainbows, and the smile on my child's face. Help me to start my days surrounded by, and deeply aware of, Your goodness.

No Nails!

Let the beauty of the LORD our God be upon us, and establish the work of our hands for us; yes, establish the work of our hands.

PSALM 90:17 NKJV

If your walls could speak, they might be shouting for a bit of color, life, and style. A great way to add these elements is with paintings and photographs. But if you don't want to put nail holes in your stone fireplace or newly painted walls, hang decorations from the ceiling. That's right! Simply install a small hook in the ceiling and use thin wire, plastic fishing line, or even silk cording. You can easily hang your favorite picture or mirror this way. Larger items can simply be leaned on the mantel. The same thing applies to your walls. Borrow a tip from your great-grandmother. Hang pictures from a cord attached at ceiling level.

One of my favorite wall decorations is a painted wooden tray hung from the ceiling with gold silk cord tassels. What do you have in the closet or placed on a dresser that could be turned into a wall centerpiece? With this method, it is easy to change paintings or decorative pieces. Think about how God decorates your life with great beauty...your children, the smile of your spouse, your own laugh. There is so much.

Simplify! Be creative and a bit daring. You will love the results in decorating and in life.

Simple Pleasures

- Dry flowers or press them to make wonderful bookmarks and gift cards.
- Find ways to decorate your rooms so that they feel like summer.
- Have an outdoor barbeque to kick the summer off with neighbors.

Wisdom for Living

Lord, may I anchor my home with beauty just as Your beauty is an anchor for my life.

Think Fabric

Adorn yourself with majesty and splendor, and array yourself with glory and beauty.

JOB 40:10 NKJV

I don't know about you, but for me decorating can be a chore. I'll share a tip with you, though. Long ago I learned a few easy tricks to making a home more beautiful. Just as life is made richer with added texture and depth, fabric will add that same beauty to any room.

The possibilities are endless. Fabric can be a decoration in itself. An inexpensive afghan can become a wall tapestry when stretched on a frame or hung from a quilt rack. The two most obvious uses for fabric are for pillows and window coverings. Pillows are an incredible decorating tool, and they add an air of comfort to a room. Vintage linens— tea towels, lace tablecloths—are beautiful tacked onto pillows or cut into curtains and draped over valance poles. Old hankies from an antique store make lovely, romantic napkins to use with your fine china.

Don't forget to add fabric to a child's room. Saving remnants of material from a child's outgrown clothes or even baby blankets can be sewn together to create a quiltlike cover for their pillows. A pattern of memories and stories is given new life with such simple steps.

Simple Pleasures

Do not stop thinking of life as an adventure.
—ELEANOR ROOSEVELT

Wisdom for Living

Lord, Your beauty adds a pattern of great beauty to our daily lives. Help me to bring a touch of that richness to my home.

Hat Tricks

Restore to me the joy of your salvation and grant me a willing spirit, to sustain me.

PSALM 51:12

In Victorian days, hats were a common adornment. They added a touch of style and provided an expression of personality for both men and women. Is there a way we can add the beauty of hats to our contemporary lives? Absolutely.

Hang a straw garden hat with gardening tools and seed packets. Or an antique bonnet hung with a little purse and maybe an antique photo. Use a hat as a "picture" inside an empty frame. Or line up several over a window. It's so much fun once you start coming up with your own ideas as well. I've put straw hats in a corner or on a table. Decorate them with silk flowers and hang on a door. Use an upside-down straw hat as a basket to hold a plant or even a crock of dip. These are the kinds of touches that give your home a hint of "you"!

Perhaps this decorating tip will even inspire you to add hats back into your wardrobe. You might be surprised how they complete the look of an Easter outfit or a simple black evening dress. While hats are not used in everyday attire, they can add such a sense of fun and refinement. You might even start a fashion trend among your group of friends!

Simple Pleasures

- Make room for hats in your life. Invite friends over for a hat party on the patio.
- Spend the morning listening to the birds. Hum along to their songs of joy.
- Fill your lungs with fresh air this morning. Thank the Lord for the day.

Wisdom for Living

Lord, let me count the ways You have made me an individual.
And let me celebrate my personal style and the character
You have given me from the day I was born.

A Miniature Work of Art

Give unto the LORD the glory due to His name; worship the LORD in the beauty of holiness.

PSALM 29:2 NKJV

When I look out at an ocean view or at a meadow of wildflowers, a sense of calm comes over me. Have you experienced that very thing? The view is beautiful because it is simple, uncluttered, and inviting. A clean line of hills against the morning sky. Or the squiggle of the water's edge playing on the sand. And when we look more closely at such a scene, we take in the other elements that add to the picture. A piece of driftwood just to the right seems to point to the sky. A patch of blue delphiniums adds dimension as a backdrop to the gentle green of sage. Soon a simple scene unfolds as a cleverly detailed masterpiece.

These same inviting scenes can be a part of your home environment. All it takes is a little imagination. For example, take any flat surface in your home and create a "tablescape." This is simply an artfully arranged group of items that otherwise jumble up on top of the dresser. Group these "necessaries" along with lovely accents, and you will create a pleasing combination on your dresser. You might try utilizing grandfather's old watch, a hand-painted oil lamp, or a small cluster of photos. How about a vase full of antique hatpins, a round bowl of mixed flowers, or a silk scarf draped over the mirror? If you can pull it off, it will improve the view in your rooms. And it takes "clutter" to a new level of sophistication—from just random pieces to a lovingly designed masterpiece!

Simple Pleasures

- Make paper dolls with your little girl and her friends.
- Go visit a neighbor's new puppy.
- Watch the sun go down. Pray over your family in the stillness.

Wisdom for Living

*Dear Father, You inspire the creativity in my soul.
I see Your amazing touches in the simplest of landscapes,
and they give me such joy. Thank You for caring
about every little detail that fills the earth.*

Reflections of Beauty

The man who looks intently into the perfect law that gives freedom, and continues to do this, not forgetting what he has heard, but doing it—he will be blessed in what he does.

JAMES 1:25

Space and beauty. When you add these two elements to a room, they can change the feel from cramped to comfortable, from blah to breathtaking. And you can do this with an item that is so easy to find, you might have looked right into one this morning.

Mirrors are wonderful decorating tools. Use them all over your house! For example, lean an interestingly framed mirror inside a window to disguise a less-than-perfect view. Include framed mirrors in a wall arrangement. Place one on a coffee table, and select three or four items to arrange on top of it for an organized visual arrangement that adds a serene touch. Use old mirrored trays, department-store framed mirrors, or hardware-store mirrored tiles as place mats. Here's another idea: Hang pictures on a large mirror with fishing wire attached to the ceiling molding. The pictures look like they're floating in midair. Or hang a mirror from an old dresser over a fireplace. In other words, expand your visual space!

Best of all, mirrors are a simple reminder that we are a reflection of the image of God. Let the atmosphere of your home always reflect the inner loveliness of your Creator.

Simple Pleasures

- Have a makeover party with friends as an excuse to laugh and relax.
- Schedule a manicure and go with a friend.
- Think about hanging that oval mirror horizontally for a different look.

Wisdom for Living

My Lord, please make my home a reflection of Your goodness and peace.
When I catch a glimpse of myself in a mirror,
may I first see the child of God You created me to be.

Beauty Is Not an Option

Teach me to do your will, for you are my God; may your good Spirit lead me on level ground.

PSALM 143:10

Sharing God's love is a blessing. And your home is one of the most tangible ways to showcase the beauty of God's love to your family. Beauty is not optional in a loving, comfortable home. It springs forth naturally when you spend time on little, extra, simple touches.

Beauty has a lot of faces! It can be found in a photograph or a hand-stitched quilt. Or in shelves lined with bright-colored jelly jars. Beauty can be a pot of ivy or a sweet potato vine growing in a jar. Even the arrangement of your home can be beautiful. When furniture and objects are combined with care and attention, the result can be warm and attractive. Some morning after the kids are at school, napping, or busy playing, give yourself 15 minutes to fiddle with the arrangement of your furniture. Even if you just focus on one piece, you will be amazed at how different the room will look as that chair, buffet, or end table makes its way into various locations. At the end of that few minutes, decide on one of the new positions for the piece of furniture. Try it out for a week. See how it feels. Is it inviting? Pleasing to the eye? Does it welcome you to enter that room and stay awhile?

What is beautiful to you? What makes you smile? What makes your spirit soar? That's the kind of beauty that should surround you in your home. Discover it and then share it with others.

Simple Pleasures

A thing of beauty is a joy forever; its loveliness increases;
it can never pass into nothingness.
—JOHN KEATS

Wisdom for Living

Thank You, Lord, for the many blessings I have. May I share them with others and may I celebrate the beauty of change every day.

Old-Fashioned Charm

Into your hands I commit my spirit; redeem me, O LORD, the God of truth.

PSALM 31:5

The days of twirling a parasol in the afternoon sunshine might be gone, but old-fashioned charm can be a way of life, a chosen style for even contemporary living. Old-fashioned may sometimes seem out of place in today's up-to-the-minute society, but when we cut through the urgency of life, the things that really matter are, well, old-fashioned—love, family, friends, faith, and a place to call home.

Your home can radiate this desired charm without requiring a lot of money. Handmade items—wall hangings, pillows—are wonderful for creating a warm, personal look. If you're not a craftsy person, check out craft sales and consignment shops. Put a series of your children's crayon drawings in matching frames. Hang them on the wall of your kitchen or hallway. For a touch of old-fashioned charm, try "dressing" your house for the change of seasons. When you buy furniture, use a professional to help you get the right basic pieces and then decorate the rest of the room on your own.

Be creative and let your individual taste show you the way! Emily Post said: "The charm of a house, like the charm of a person, is an outward manifestation of inward grace!" Oh, I just love that.

Simple Pleasures

* Bake a spice cake and enjoy the wonderful aroma in your home.
* Start a batch of homemade popsicles to beat the heat.
* Have fresh water with lemon available for the kids to drink all day.

Wisdom for Living

Lord, there is nothing old-fashioned about loving You!
Your presence fills my home with beauty, energy, and charm.
Gracious living is all about showing Your grace.

House-warmings

O LORD, you have searched me and you know me…you are familiar with all my ways.

PSALM 139:1,3

There is such comfort in knowing God cares about every little detail in our lives. From our worries about our children to our joy in creating a garden of beauty, He is paying attention.

You can offer your family and yourself this same attention. With a quick survey of your house or apartment, see what simple changes or additions will reflect a heart and mind for loving detail.

If you're lucky enough to have a fireplace, make it a focus of your room. With a little decoration, it can be an eye-catching highlight of your living area. For me, there's something about a rocking chair that encourages people to sit and talk. A favorite stuffed toy, a framed picture, and any memento that touches you can make your home look warmer and cozier. Christmas pictures at Christmas and vacation pictures in the summer make your home a changing seasonal gallery! You can never have enough pillows. They're wonderful for decoration. Many people find a puzzle irresistible. Or try using a sturdy wooden trunk for a coffee table.

Creativity is really just a knack for noticing ways to beautify an environment. I know *you* are creative! How do I know? Because I have met your heavenly Father.

Simple Pleasures

- Plan a neighborhood beach party in your yard. Decorate with beach balls and tiki torches.
- Make hamburgers and hot dogs and serve them up on red plates.
- Have a sprinkler going and play beach-themed music.

Wisdom for Living

*Create in me a clean spirit, O Lord. Give me, I pray,
an eye for beauty. A heart for joy. And a mind for loving You.*

Bits and Pieces

When my spirit grows faint within me, it is you who know my way.

PSALM 142:3

Have you noticed that life is one big interesting mosaic in process? We use odds and ends from others to create the life that is ours. We gather ideas from a friend. We recall recipes from a relative. We add new finds to heirlooms to create a home we love. So don't ever overlook bits and pieces. They might be the perfect next addition to your life.

Real treasures are the bits and pieces you can transform into loved possessions for your home. Pick up single lids and stoppers or teapots without lids. You may find that two "orphans" fit each other. If not, they make great Christmas ornaments. Old, beat-up, gold-leaf frames are a prize! Patch the molding with chewing gum and re-spray the gold. Old costume jewelry is great for children. They love it for dress up. Even broken jewelry can be used for crafting future treasures. Odd drawers from broken pieces can be used as file boxes, flower boxes, and letter trays. Be quick to pounce on cabinets, trunks, and cases that can be put to different uses. The only limit is your imagination!

Just think about how God is piecing together your life. A little of this. A little of that. Have fun following this recipe for creating a life that transforms fragments into a whole work of art.

Simple Pleasures

- Take broken or chipped plates or cups and make a mosaic tabletop or mirror frame.
- Look around you. Who is hurting and needs a prayer for healing and wholeness?
- Give your hurts and broken pieces to God and watch something beautiful emerge.

Wisdom for Living

You piece my life together, Lord. I offer You brokenness and You mend me. I offer You disorder and You make it all fit. What a lesson in true beauty!

Sparkles and Beads

It shone with the glory of God, and its brilliance was like that of a very precious jewel, like a jasper, clear as crystal.

REVELATION 21:11-12

Make the rooms you live in a feast for the eyes. They will lift your spirits throughout the days. Inexpensive ideas are great...and cheap ones are even better! Add some pizzazz and nobody has to know.

For example, who'd ever guess that your striking sideboard is plywood set on sawhorses? Add a patterned cloth and some colorful flowers. You've got yourself a conversation piece at very little cost. Or line your old hutch with fabric. It will make a wonderful backdrop for your prized pottery or china. Jazz up just about any area of your home with a pile of wonderful pillows. You can even add some fringe or sparkling beads. They are so popular right now and you can find everything you need either at a fabric store or by rummaging through a garage sale. Look for old jewelry—you'll never run out of a need for "sparkles and beads"! Place new or old beads and pieces of jewelry (this is especially good for broken pieces) in a little glass fishbowl and set it on top of a small mirror in the middle of a windowsill. Stand back and watch the light dance!

Simple Pleasures

* Dazzle a room by using the light. Incorporate mirrors, stained glass, and old beads.
* Intertwine silver ribbon in a bowl of red glass rocks for a sparkling centerpiece.
* Arrange vases to catch the light. They can be remarkable with or without flowers.

Wisdom for Living

Dear God, please remind me daily that a forgiven heart shines like rays of sunlight. May I decorate my home with the brilliance of such beauty as a reminder of this newness, this gift of light in my life.

Enough Beauty to Go Around

*Blessed are the poor in spirit, for
theirs is the kingdom of heaven.*

MATTHEW 5:3

Other than wishing our bathrooms were self-cleaning, how much thought do we really give them? Maybe it is time to give this room some attention. It is the one room in the house that everyone uses. And, thankfully, it's one of the simplest rooms to make wonderful changes to with a touch of old-fashioned luxury!

I don't know about you, but I love monogrammed towels. Watch for sales and you can indulge yourself quite economically. Try attaching a dried-flower rose bouquet to a towel rack. It adds just the right touch of inexpensive "luxury." If you have room for a chair, add a colorful pillow or chair back to it. Add some matching touches with the soap dish or a vase. If you have wall space, hang several decorative mirrors, sconces with candles, and framed pictures to warm up a room that often feels sterile or merely functional at best. There is no reason to ignore your home's overall style when you get to the bathroom.

And of course, baskets, baskets, baskets. Use as many as you can for extra storage space for towels, washcloths, and soaps.

Simple Pleasures

- Buy scented soaps and tuck them in drawers until you use them.
- Make book covers out of waterproof material for bathtime reading.
- Get monogrammed towels for your children so they can keep track of their own linens.

Wisdom for Living

*Lord, You have washed away my sins. You make me clean and new.
I think of this blessing today and thank You for Your grace.*

Need a Face-Lift?

The Spirit gives life; the flesh counts for nothing. The words I have spoken to you are spirit and they are life.

JOHN 6:63

"If I could only have a better nose, a tuck here and there, blonde hair. If I could only be more like 'so and so,' I would be okay as a person." Do thoughts like this echo in your mind? Do you have a list you hold in your heart of all the things wrong with you? Well, friend, it is time to dump those negative thoughts. They can poison your system. We can't be lifted up when we spend so much time tearing ourselves down.

One child, two children, three children later...and you might not have the flat stomach you had before bearing children. Does it matter? Really matter? Look at your children. Would you do it all over again? Then stop hurting yourself by being such a critic. What you might not yet notice is how your attitude can begin to impact your children. Your negative thoughts about body image is teaching them a value you will wish they did not inherit.

Do you realize that God made you uniquely different from everyone else? Yes, it's important to work on improving imperfections, but don't dwell on them so much that you forget who you are in His sight. Go easy on yourself. The way we'll improve our self-image is by being positive and acknowledging that we are God's cherished creation!

Simple Pleasures

* Look in the mirror and tell God what you love about your face and body.
* Start walking to increase your physical and mental energy. Feel great about yourself.
* Begin each day with five minutes of stretching. You will stand taller and feel better.

Wisdom for Living

Father, I come to You ashamed, not of my body but of my attitude toward it. Help me accept all of me...the me You created. I will love myself and take care of myself each day.

July

Rest and Renewal

Lightening Our Loads

> May your unfailing love rest upon us, O LORD, even as we put our hope in you.
>
> PSALM 33:22

When you are in the middle of praying for an extra pair of hands to tidy the kitchen, feed the baby, or call parents for the car pool, it is so easy to forget about the help we are given as Christians. The power that runs the universe is available to us—if we're humble enough to accept it. What an incredible thought!

So why do we keep staggering under loads of guilt, worry, or laundry? Why fret over how much we have to do when a source of power is promised us? Often it is merely a case of pride. We'd rather break our backs doing it our way than admit the load's too heavy. Isn't that silly? Listen to what God says: "Come to Me, all you who labor and are heavy laden, and I will give you rest" (Matthew 11:28 NKJV). God is saying, "I've got work for you to do—important work." Your role as a parent is of great importance. Motherhood requires commitment, strength, a good sense of humor, and reliance on God.

Today, you have a big job ahead of you. It might not go as planned. But remember that in God's design, it's never more than we can handle—with His help. Ask Him. Humbly ask the Lord to be your source of help.

Simple Pleasures

* Laugh about something you did wrong today. Trade guilt for joy.
* Play some Christmas music. Let words celebrating the birth of Christ sink into your heart and soothe your soul.
* Enjoy some hot cider or tea while writing a note to a friend.

Wisdom for Living

I seek Your help today, Lord. You are my strength and the source of my joy each day. Thank You for Your ever-present help.

Celebrate God

> The whole earth is at rest and quiet; they break forth into singing.
>
> ISAIAH 14:7 NKJV

Do you long for quiet time with the Lord? In our busy days, this oasis can seem like a luxury, but really it is a way to nourish your soul. And your quiet time is not a gift you give to God—it's a gift God gives to you! And when you do make quiet time a practice in your day-to-day life, you realize what an exceptional gift it is!

Simply offer Him your time and yourself. He's the One who will provide the quiet spirit. Get in the habit of saying, "Good morning, Lord" and "Good evening, Lord." Start and end each day with some time of simply being with God. Wait just a minute before you bring Him all your wants and concerns. Remember to be thankful for the prayers He's already answered. Use this motto: Praise before prayer! Be courageous in your asking and confident in His answers. But first—have the privilege of celebrating God's presence. His very faithfulness is a promise and a blessing all wrapped in one!

Sometimes it's hard to accept the gifts we need most. Unwrap the ribbons of grace and the wrappings of peace and receive the gift God has chosen for you today in your time with Him.

Simple Pleasures

- Break forth into song! Try it when no one else is around.
- After a good stretch, try a cartwheel or give a hula hoop a try.
- Take a power walk and return for a glass of fresh juice.

Wisdom for Living

Lord, You give me so much. My time in Your presence renews me.
Thank You for being there when I call on Your name.

Make It a Special Place

When you lie down, you will not be afraid; when you lie down, your sleep will be sweet.

PROVERBS 3:24

Sweet dreams begin with a bedroom that is designed for a good night's sleep. Make that bedroom of yours a special place. Take a close look at it and describe the feeling it gives. Is it soothing? Is it cheery? Is it cluttered? The bedroom is one of the most important places to simplify and create a calming atmosphere.

I know I just told you to simplify, but one piece worth adding is a pillow. Well, make that pillows, pillows, pillows! Honestly, you can't have enough of them for a warm, cozy effect.

Be a little daring. Stitch beads (in any color you like) to curtains as tiebacks or trim. Add a colorful shade to your lamp and let the colors glow all over the room. Hang a tote from a bedpost for books, magazines, Bible, or journal. And get rid of the dresser-top clutter! Use a painted tray or a mirror. Add some flowers in an old pottery jar. Put your pictures in some nice new frames to match your décor. Make your bedroom a place you enjoy, a place that expresses your unique personality and creativity. And, if you're married, don't forget your husband. Let his personality come shining through as well. Work on it together and create a real sanctuary for the two of you.

Simple Pleasures

* Fluff up your pillows every other day and let fresh air into the bedroom.
* Use a scented carpet freshener in your room to bring in the ambience of a floral meadow.
* Pull out photos of when you and your husband first dated, and put them up in the bedroom.

Wisdom for Living

Lord, You created sleep to give us daily renewal. That is such a gift for me. I pray that my bedroom would be a place of Your peace.

Cut the Clutter

You gave abundant showers, O God; you refreshed your weary inheritance.

PSALM 68:9

Sometimes we aren't even aware we're surrounded by clutter. And there are many different kinds. Today, I want to focus on "time" clutter. Do you do things over and over again that could be simplified with a little advance planning? Cut out this kind of clutter in your life.

First of all, determine what's important. That's where a good "to do" list comes in handy. It keeps you from getting off track. Here's an idea I really like. Instead of handwriting a shopping list every week, make a list of stuff you typically buy. Print a bunch of copies and stick one on your refrigerator. Just circle items as you need them. Leave a space to write in the additional items. If you're buying a birthday card, buy several to use over the next few months. Break down big tasks into smaller ones. It's those big items that will throw you.

What's the point of all this? The way life works, when you remove one activity from your schedule, something else will immediately fill the void. That is just the way it is. So this exercise in cutting out the clutter of repetitive tasks is to make room for prayer time, family time, or personal time. Make room for the abundance of important blessings in your life, like children, laughter, family, and memories.

Simple Pleasures

- Go through your kitchen cupboards. Start left to right and get rid of things you don't use.
- Do you notice the same grocery items growing old or stale? Stop buying them.
- Buy some pressed fruit treats instead of cookies for your children's snacks.

Wisdom for Living

I want all my time to really count for You, Lord.
What takes away from the time I could be spending with You?
Show me where I can make positive changes in my schedule.

Set the Clock Back

He will renew your life and sustain you in your old age.

As women we hear all about "setting the clock back." But this is not a quick fix for smoothing out fine lines and wrinkles. This is about gleaning more time out of your day by not wasting moments that could be saved up for a useful, soothing chunk of time later on. Wouldn't it be nice to give yourself an extra hour a day?

I have a friend that's constantly late for appointments. To ease my own frustration, I always give her a time that's 15 minutes earlier than I need her to be there. It works! Do the same thing at home. Set your clocks five to ten minutes ahead of the correct time. Here's another stress saver. Rather than nag your children five minutes before they leave for school, set a small alarm clock to go off five minutes before they're to leave. Who knows, maybe eventually they'll get the idea.

To save your sanity, make a "to do" list for the next day before you go to bed. It will give you a jump start on tomorrow. Also, writing the list down helps you release those worries from your mind so that you can say your evening prayers and drift off to sleep without rehashing your schedule in the morning. You will start the next day much more refreshed.

Simple Pleasures

- Don't wear a watch all day and just go with the flow for once.
- Make a clock! Craft stores have the supplies for an easy project to do with the family.
- Simplify your life in every way you can. This adds time and quality!

Wisdom for Living

O God, sometimes I feel as though I am spinning my wheels.
Show me how to calm my spirit and make wise decisions.
Let me be a good steward with the precious gift of time.

*Find rest, O my soul, in God
alone; my hope comes from him.*

PSALM 62:5

You don't need a lot of people to enjoy a lovely tea party! A tea can provide an opportunity for great fellowship, but taking tea alone is a celebration you definitely don't want to miss.

Take the time in a long afternoon to prepare a lovely tea and just pamper yourself. Or if you have the luxury of an evening alone, why not prepare tea with fruit and sandwiches around 5:00 and enjoy the quiet nighttime hours?

A simple menu for your solitary tea is easy, healthy, and satisfying. First, the perfect pot of tea. Add orange or apple slices to your plate. Make cream cheese, celery, and walnut sandwiches, and top it all off with some homemade cookies. Lay a pretty cloth on a tray or table and add a flower or candle for some elegance. Then sit down in your cozy spot, have your tea, and enjoy some time alone with God.

These preparations don't have to be extravagant. They are just a way of celebrating time in God's presence. This practice will bring you great joy. If you have a friend who also could use a break, you might suggest that you each indulge in a personal afternoon tea while the other one watches the children for a few hours. Now that is simply a divine way to spend the day.

Simple Pleasures

There are few hours in my life more agreeable than
the hour dedicated to the ceremony known as afternoon tea.

—HENRY JAMES

Wisdom for Living

*Refreshment for my soul includes time alone with You, God.
My cup is filled with new strength, hope, and faith. This is a good day.*

Quality Time Alone

He makes me lie down in green pastures, he leads me beside quiet waters, he restores my soul.

PSALM 23:2-3

When was the last time you had some quality alone time? If it is taking awhile to recall such a moment, it's definitely time to schedule in some personal time. Your life is too busy to not have some quiet moments to yourself.

A friend of mine attended an expensive seminar and learned: 1) Make a "to do" list (I could have told her that!) and 2) schedule quality time alone each day. It doesn't have to be a large block of time. Fifteen minutes here and there can do wonders. Ask a neighbor to watch the kids for 15 minutes while you sprinkle a few bath crystals in the tub and enjoy the solitude. Stake out a table in a coffee shop or park your car under a tree. Enjoy a time of quiet with the Lord. Schedule longer quiet times too. Study your Bible, pray, write in your journal, read a book—refresh your mind and restore your soul. It sounds simple enough, doesn't it? Then why don't we do it more often? You need to first consider this time a priority in your life. Let yourself do that. Your family, friends, coworkers, and whoever interacts with you will notice the difference and will enjoy the more relaxed version of you.

Simple Pleasures

- Encourage your children to enjoy alone time. It will develop their minds and interests.
- Choose an evening each week to set a curfew on noise so your home is calm before bed.
- Have a family bedtime reading circle.

Wisdom for Living

Don't let me run from alone time, Lord.
It is essential to the well-being of my spirit.
Help me find ways to seek solitude and moments of peace.

Make Yourself at Home

Then, because so many people were coming and going that they did not even have a chance to eat, he said to them, "Come with me by yourselves to a quiet place and get some rest."

MARK 6:31

"Come on in and make yourself at home!" Don't you just love to hear those words?

When you make yourself at home, you surround yourself with the people you love, objects you cherish, memories that warm you. You work to create a place where you can rest and be renewed. Look around you right now. Do you feel a sense of renewal? Are you warmed by the objects and colors that surround you? If not, you are in for a treat! Let's focus on a few priorities and create a place that embraces you with a spirit of hospitality.

Invest time, care, and loving energy to keeping your nest clean and warm and welcoming. Protect your home from the clutter of neglect. I don't mean your home has to be perfect. We need to get past that. Your home just needs to be loving and filled with the personal beauty only you can offer. From there, it's a natural! Other people will feel at home as well. Just open your heart and adjust your living space to make room for one more person—or a few—or a dozen!

Simple Pleasures

- Keep snack foods on hand for unexpected guests—cheese, crackers, iced tea.
- Invite a single man or woman from your church to dinner.
- Ask a new neighbor to join you for a cup of coffee.

Wisdom for Living

How does my home express me? Or You, Lord?
I want to do both…and I want a place where
my family feels truly at home.

Something New from Something Old

And He said, "My Presence will go with you, and I will give you rest."

EXODUS 33:14 NKJV

Create something new from something old! Reinvent a piece of furniture. Splash on a glaze color to give it a fresh, subtle charm. Do you have an old plate or bowl? Use it to decorate a wall or hold a planter. A collection of flowerpots can hold candles or potpourri. A child's wagon can become an outdoor planter. Or take that rusty old mailbox. Scrape it and paint it—or even add some decoupage because the "crackle" look is back—and it's more popular than ever!

Are you thinking of some items? There are so many ideas to consider. If you've saved those old TV trays—and they're not worth taking to the Antique Road Show—paint them. Use them to display photos or books. Use your imagination! Start with one room and incorporate a theme. Use red, white, and blue touches to create an Americana feel. Place old family photos on the wall. What was once just a spare room or a workroom with plain walls is now a legacy room.

We just have to look at "stuff" with new eyes. It's really a simple way to add some refreshment to your home and to infuse your surroundings with God's presence. Make His heart known in every room.

Simple Pleasures

- Place baskets on the wall for variety.
- Put up a couple shelves to set framed photos on. Lean the photos on the wall.
- Take an old lamp and let it be a centerpiece whether it works or not!

Wisdom for Living

Lord, You saw in my broken heart something new and whole.
You created a place to fill with the treasures of faith and love.

If Only I Had Time for Me

He gives strength to the weary and increases the power of the weak.

ISAIAH 40:29

I've had so many women express to me, "If only I had time for myself." How often do you catch yourself saying this very thing throughout the day? Well, it is up to you to make that happen, and here are some encouraging ways to spend time on yourself.

Have your hair and nails done. Read a book on nutrition and change your eating habits. Take a stroll on the beach or in the park. Listen to good music. Spend time alone. Too many women neglect that simple concept of time alone with themselves and with God. Yet, isn't it what your heart is yearning for? If this longing is ignored for too long, you will find that the other time is spent spinning your wheels. You won't have focus or stamina. And your heart won't be in your activities.

So list everything you're thankful for. Or have a good cry! You've earned it. Visit a friend. Buy flowers for yourself. Serve someone in need. Read the Psalms—they're God's little painkillers! The bottom line: Learn to care for yourself. Hey, it's okay. In fact, it is more than okay, it is God's gift to you.

Simple Pleasures

- Tell your children that you want quiet time for an hour. Set a timer and enjoy.
- Feel free to take a nap when your young children are doing the same. Work can wait.
- Get up just a little earlier than the children so that you start your day with the Lord!

Wisdom for Living

I am drawn to Your heart, Lord. This time I seek to spend by myself and in Your presence will make me a healthier, happier, more centered woman of God.

Your Dream Bedroom

He who dwells in the shelter of the Most High will rest in the shadow of the Almighty.

Today let's dream a bit and see what we can do to spruce up your bedroom. You can add some pizzazz with some really easy projects.

Old doors and even shutters make fascinating headboards. An old iron bed frame is a real find in a junk or antique store. Try red gloss enamel for a teenager's room or matte black with gold highlights for a sophisticated guest bedroom. For a child's room, paint the letters of their name on the headboard or write a bedtime prayer using a fine paintbrush.

In your room, cover the wall behind the bed with fabric instead of using a headboard. This is a soft, attractive look that can be changed so easily, even season to season. And almost any small piece of furniture can become a nightstand. A tea cart of wood or wicker, or a cloth draped over a round side table from Kmart, works great! Keep the lighting soft and use a floor lamp or table lamp beside a reading table. See! Now you've got the start of a "dreamy" bedroom. May it lead you to rest in the Lord each night and help you begin each day with the security of His goodness.

Simple Pleasures

- Wear a dress today if you usually wear pants or vice versa.
- Go card shopping on your lunch break and think of people to keep in touch with.
- Eat one of those wonderful large soft pretzels.

Wisdom for Living

God, please protect my family while they sleep.
Guard their dreams. Let them wake up with
thoughts of thanksgiving to You for a new day.

Take Care of Yourself

The Sovereign LORD has given me an instructed tongue, to know the word that sustains the weary. He wakens me morning by morning, wakens my ear to listen like one being taught.

ISAIAH 50:4

Is life crazy? This might be the day for some simple ideas to save your sanity!

You might want to begin by spending some time alone. Read a good book. Listen to music. Here are my favorites—get a professional massage or have your nails done. And *don't feel guilty.* You're not making a career out of this. We're talking about taking care of yourself so you can be better equipped to do what God has for you. For some moms, just a chance to take a long bath in solitude is a pampered moment. Or how about a long walk alone on a fall afternoon, taking in the varying hues of autumn and talking to God. These are important things to do!

While you are talking to Him, listen to Him. God has words to ease your soul.

And now that the guilt is out of the way for the moment, let me continue with this wonderful list: Spend a weekend with your husband in a quiet setting. Use it as a time to regroup physically and spiritually. Buy a bouquet of flowers for *you!* Serve a friend in need. Make a date with girlfriends. Or plan an afternoon or evening to call a few friends who live far away.

Do you get the pattern here? Simple ideas. Simply relaxing.

Simple Pleasures

- Mentally squish guilt when it enters your mind. You are too busy to play that game.
- Use language that does not create guilt for others. Serve them with kindness.
- If guilt still enters the picture, write the situation down on paper and use it for kindling.

Wisdom for Living

Merciful God of comfort, I praise You. I am deeply grateful that You care so deeply about my well-being. I want to be healthy in every way.

Summertime Projects

Unless the LORD builds the house,
its builders labor in vain.

PSALM 127:1

"There's nothing to do, Mom!" Sound familiar? I can offer you a few quick tips for summertime projects to keep children busy. Busy children are a great thing. Follow some of these suggestions, and maybe make yourself an idea notebook for this very thing. Each summer you will be glad to have ideas at your fingertips.

While adults often lose this passion, most kids love rocks. Have them pick up their favorite shapes and then paint them with flowers, people, or animals. One summer our children filled their wagons with rocks and sold them to our neighbors as paperweights. Or have your children choose a recipe and make something from scratch. Take pictures and put together a summer scrapbook. Have them write down notes to go with the photos to create a summer family journal. Won't that be great to look at later in life!

Plant and care for a vegetable or flower garden. Children love to watch plants come up. Or have them press wildflowers to use for art projects or for Christmas cards later on. Psalm 127:3 says: "Children are a gift from God; they are his reward" (TLB). Spend time with your kiddos—they are so worthwhile.

Simple Pleasures

- Make a date with each child this week and choose something simple and fun to do.
- Walk barefoot in your yard for an evening. Feel the soil between your toes.
- Make homemade lemonade and sip it while reading your Bible in the evening.

Wisdom for Living

Lord, children are such a gift. They not only add richness to my life,
they show me a pure heart and a giving spirit.

Summer Party

The heartfelt counsel of a friend is as sweet as perfume.

PROVERBS 29:9 NLT

While the kids are splashing in the community pool this summer, make your own splash with a festive, relaxing, summer tea party for friends.

Beautifully selected glasses with icy cold tea served to friends on a summer afternoon is a great way to celebrate friendship. What would you do without those chosen sisters who laugh with you, cry with you, and speak truth to you? And what better way to celebrate your friendship than with the intimacy of a "friendship tea"?

Select the kind of food you like best. Order it in or choose a menu you can prepare a day ahead. That way you are relaxed and getting into the spirit of a soothing tea before your friends arrive. You will greet each guest with a calm manner instead of the intensity that comes from last-minute rushing. Music from a CD player in the background works great. A friend recently had a tea in the garden of her home to celebrate her own successful gardening efforts. Her favorite friends were invited for the celebration of her efforts and blessings. Tea is as much about friendship as it is about tea! Get those invitations ready and let your friends know how special they are in your life.

Simple Pleasures

- Create a place in your home where you can be alone to read, pray, or just think quietly.
- Set a chair in your yard in the shade so you have a pleasant place to relax during a hot day.
- Plant fragrant flowers in a section of your yard and set a welcoming bench among them.

Wisdom for Living

Where two or more are gathered in Your name, Lord, You are there.
I feel Your presence when I am among my closest friends.
How grateful I am for being surrounded by love.

151

Let It Shine!

Let your face shine on your servant; save me in your unfailing love.

PSALM 31:16

"This little light of mine, I'm going to let it shine...." This sweet children's song is a reminder of the light God places in each of us. It radiates warmth and joy to everyone who stands within its glow. The lamps in our home share this same sense of warmth with our family and visitors.

Here are some ideas for creating wonderful lamps and shades to cast a gentle glow in your everyday surroundings. For a base how about a cookie jar or a teapot? A child's wooden toy? Old sports equipment? One time I even saw a lamp that was made from an old manual typewriter! And for your shades? Just glue buttons or bows onto a shade you've purchased. Antique linens are great for gathering around a shade you already have. Black lace on a black background—talk about "shady"! And your children's artwork—what a treasure.

These special "light" touches will add personal character and significance to the lamps in your home.

Simple Pleasures

- Try being a light by sending encouraging notes to children in your church's youth group.
- Sign up to help with the next mailing a local charity has scheduled.
- Get a head start on items needed for when your children go back to school.

Wisdom for Living

Lord, let my home be an example of Your light in my life.
Let the warmth of that love always radiate
from every room in the house.

A Big Bare Wall

The LORD will grant you abundant prosperity—in the fruit of your womb, the young of your livestock and the crops of your ground—in the land he swore to your forefathers to give you.

DEUTERONOMY 28:11

Remember the thrill of finger painting? Splashes of color seemed to brighten any day when creativity was let loose on a white piece of paper. Recapture that joy as an adult. Now that blank piece of paper is a white wall. Think of the possibilities with paint!

I absolutely love paint. It's such an inexpensive investment. So inexpensive you can afford to play with it! Go ahead, experiment a little! You can always paint over anything you don't like. A handy can of white paint is your eraser, just in case.

Instead of rolling a coat of paint on a wall, try sponging or stamping or even stenciling. Paint one wall a different color, or paint the bottom half a contrasting color and install a chair rail where the colors meet. If you're truly original, grab your paintbrush and try some freehand designs. The point is to be creative as you put your own loving touches throughout your home. Even get the kids to join you. Let them do some experimenting in their rooms—under supervision, of course!

Color reflects the personalities within a home. Get everyone in on the act. And when the seasons change, and you are looking for a makeover in your home, take an inspirational tour through the color sample section of a home improvement store. The possibilities are endless.

Simple Pleasures

- Paint a rainbow on your child's wall or in the children's bathroom.
- Hang flat metallic ornaments shaped like stars and angels along a hallway wall.
- Place a chime near your favorite garden spot and listen to the wind sing.

Wisdom for Living

Lord, You painted the rainbow as a symbol of Your promise to us. May I express my promise to make a lovely, lively home for my family with the joy of color.

The Personal Art of Collecting

> By wisdom a house is built, and through understanding it is established; through knowledge its rooms are filled with rare and beautiful treasures.
>
> PROVERBS 24:4

What are the special little somethings that give you joy? Do you have a collection of small or large treasures? You can receive so much happiness by surrounding yourself with images, items, shapes, and colors that you love. For example, one teacup is simply a teacup! Two teacups is service for two. But if you take your teacups, arrange them on a shelf with a lace scarf, and perhaps add a third to keep them company, you have something that brightens your living space. You have the beginnings of a collection.

I know a man who collects university T-shirts. A couple I met in Kansas collect old buggies and sleighs. Another friend's bookmark collection is kept in an old shoebox. A collection is as unique as your personality. It could begin with an heirloom—a stamp collection. Collections can also spark an interest in children to learn about a new subject. Include your children in the research about your collected item or encourage them to select their own collections of interest and watch the fun begin. Something as simple as a seashell or rock collection can provide years of entertainment for a child.

I guarantee your collection will become a way of expressing yourself, and best of all, a way to share yourself, your values, and your faith.

Simple Pleasures

* Collect your child's laughter. See how many times you can hear it today.
* Think about adding to someone's special collection as a surprise.
* Give away collections that you or your children don't care for anymore.

Wisdom for Living

Lord, let my pursuits lead to sharing about my life, my faith, and the interests You have blessed me with.

Letter Writing and Journals

You yourselves are our letter, written on our hearts, known and read by everybody.

2 CORINTHIANS 3:2

Old-fashioned? That's me! And do you know why? Because some of the simplest yet most profound ideas are quite old-fashioned. But once they are tried, they blend wonderfully with a modern life. Just wait and see.

A fine example is letter writing. I know, in this day of e-mail it's a lost art. But what a wonderful way of building relationships and preserving our words for future generations. And by the way, the Bible is a great example of "preserving words" for all generations! So is the practice of writing in diaries and journals. We give a gift of memory to the next generation when we keep a chronicle of our "everydays." When you go on a trip, send yourself a postcard or two as a way to preserve a moment and chronicle an adventure. Write your children letters to tell them about something they did that made you smile. Write letters to the Lord as a family or keep a "Dear God" journal.

Preserving a written memory takes time and space and effort. But it can be eminently worthwhile. So many tales my mother told me have already dimmed in my memory. I've all but forgotten some of them, and she's not here to ask anymore. If you can, make the time to create a record of your family stories. You'll be glad you did.

Simple Pleasures

- Pick out a special pen for letter writing and for journaling. You will love the feel of it.
- Plan a date with each of your children so they can go pick out a journal and a pen.
- Create a photo journal. Take a photo a week and place it in a notebook.

Wisdom for Living

Your Word is written upon my heart, Lord. Let it be written on my life as well. Let me chronicle Your many blessings and Your faithfulness as I record my days.

More Fun, Less Stuff

I know what it is to be in need, and I know what it is to have plenty. I have learned the secret of being content in any and every situation, whether well fed or hungry, whether living in plenty or in want.

PHILIPPIANS 4:12

Did you know that passing on a simplified life is now a movement? A lifestyle parents are teaching their children to embrace? *Time* magazine reported "simplicity circles" popping up all across the country. The groups are advocating "more fun, less stuff." One director said, "This isn't just about unspoiling kids. It's about reclaiming our kids from a commercial culture that has spun out of control." I couldn't agree more.

One woman talks about excessive birthday parties—"over the top," as she described it. She and her husband said their kids would be just as happy playing hide-and-seek with a few friends and then having cake and ice cream. "I realized I wasn't doing this for him," she said, "I was doing it for me!"

Have you given yourself over to this same pressure? It is so easy to focus on keeping up with the chosen style of others that soon you think it is the only way to raise a family or celebrate a birthday. Does it really reflect the life you want for your family? Chances are it is creating more tension and less fulfillment for you and your children. Look around you. Parents are raising a generation of children who will never be satisfied, fulfilled, or content unless they "have it all." Give some thought to making your life a little simpler.

Simple Pleasures

* Do you have blankets you never use? Wash them and donate them to a shelter.
* Have each child decorate a file box for storing school papers.
* Make a box for yourself. You might have projects to keep this year too.

Wisdom for Living

What are my motives for spoiling my child? Do I long to see him smile?
Do I go over the top so that she will be accepted?
So that I will be accepted? Lord, help me model
a life that impresses You and You alone.

A Legacy of Love

Blessed are those who dwell in your house; they are ever praising you.

PSALM 84:4

I know you have a lot to do, but I have an idea that can turn into something wonderful for everyone. Let's plan a tea party for a young person in your life! It can all be done simply and still be sensational. It's so much fun to watch precious children enjoy a tea party. I love the thought that I'm building memories for them. But a tea party can do so much more. You're teaching basic skills of hospitality and etiquette that will serve your children well later in life.

Involve the children in every aspect so they learn about planning, baking, preparing tea, and decorating a table. They will discover why it is kind to say "please" and "thank you." They also learn that worthwhile things in life take a little effort, a little finesse. They will see that there's value in quiet things. Most of all, they will learn that they are part of a long legacy of love. The legacy of the teacup that has been placed in my hand and heart is a gift from my mother. And it's being passed on! I hope you will accept it and share the many lessons it holds.

Simple Pleasures

- Get a plastic tea set so little hands can copy what the adults are doing.
- Take a child to an antique store or flea market so they can pick out their special cup.
- Make a beautiful wall arrangement by hanging solo saucers on a kitchen wall.

Wisdom for Living

Father, I pray You would continually remind me that lessons about what is worthwhile become the cornerstone of setting priorities. Every moment I invest in my children is developing their future and their priorities for life.

Just Look Around You

O Lord Almighty, blessed is the man who trusts in you.

PSALM 84:12

I hear it all the time. "I want to be more creative, but I don't know how!" Creativity is taking simple things and bringing them to life. Trust me, you can do it. Here are some easy ideas to get you started.

Design a "love shelf" in your home to display those little gifts from friends and family that mean so much but don't fit anywhere. Take a class or workshop and learn a new skill that will help you be more creative. Schedule some time to practice your new skill—you won't become proficient in it if you don't. Use your imagination in displaying things you love—collectibles, cups and saucers, salt-and-pepper shakers. If you don't have a collection, start one. It will be so much fun!

Give yourself five minutes to list the things you would do if only you were creative. Voilà. This is really a list of all the things you *can* do. Pick a couple to try each month. If one is intimidating, ask a friend to join you for that day's project.

Just look around you. There are so many possibilities for creativity. It just takes a little practice and the courage to give things a chance.

Simple Pleasures

- You are creative. Take note of your ideas this week!
- Next time you start a project, determine not to say anything negative to yourself about it.
- Set a timer for 20 minutes and just write anything that comes to mind.

Wisdom for Living

Sometimes I don't explore my own creativity.
God, let me never doubt the spirit of creativity
that You have given me. Help me find my special gifts.

August

AMAZING ABUNDANCE

Add the Flair

Add spark to your life and everything you touch. All it takes is a little flair.

To add a bit of whimsy, use stickers or rubber stamps on your notes, letters, even your bills. Write with colored pens, use colored paper clips, and tuck in sprinkles of confetti for a festive message.

A friend's mother always encouraged her to "do whatever you do with flair!" I couldn't agree more. This includes parenting. Let your kids enjoy your personality and the expression of your creativity. Be the mom who encourages the kids to have a good time, add spark in their own endeavors, and have the courage to be themselves.

Flair can manifest itself in simple pleasures. Hang a tuneful wind chime on your patio. Dab a bit of vanilla behind your ears for a wonderful fragrance. Enjoy a bubble bath by candlelight while sipping iced tea or warm cocoa. Right now, take a few minutes and thank God for all He's done for you. Praise Him for as many things as you can think of. Have a flair for gratitude.

Simple Pleasures

* Life is abundant and rich. See it this way and embrace it fully.
* Think of ways you can make your child's life more abundant and filled with spark.
* Buy a book of plays for children and plan evenings for them to dress up for the parts.

Wisdom for Living

Father, I want to pass along to my children
an appreciation for life. I want them to experience
the joy of living fully and for You.

Think Flowers

As for man, his days are like grass, he flourishes like a flower of the field.

PSALM 103:15

Do you have a celebration coming up? Think of flowers when you think of the special days in your life—births, Easter, fall, spring, weddings—and all the moments you treasure. Adding a touch of simple beauty to your day will make a vivid memory. From the fragrance of the flower you choose to the vivid color of the petals, you will think fondly of this special day every time you experience this flower.

If you want an investment in the future, plant a tree. If you don't have a yard, consider a "green" donation to your church or even a local school. Brighten your dining room with an indoor window box. On the kitchen windowsill, put a row of herb plants. They are decorative and you can use the herbs in that gourmet meal you're whipping up this evening. Have dried flower arrangements throughout the house. Place potpourri in sachets to add fragrance to your closets and drawers.

The idea is to brighten your life with the beautiful things God has provided in nature. Thank Him for all He's done in your life, for all He provides for you to enjoy.

Simple Pleasures

- Start planning where you will want to plant bulbs in your yard.
- Peruse flower catalogs and savor the beauty of color.
- If you were a flower, what would you be?

Wisdom for Living

Oh, how Your radiance does shine in nature.
Thank You, Lord, for the blessings of color, new life,
fragrance, and design everywhere I turn.

Hidden Treasure

Blessed are those whose strength is in you, who have set their hearts on pilgrimage.

PSALM 84:5

Today we're going on a treasure hunt, and we will add some great touches to your home along the way. Ready?

Look around you. What do you see? There may be some wonderful home décor possibilities in your old stuff. Empty out those cupboards, especially the ones where you store odds and ends or boxes of items you used to use regularly. Check it out. There may be treasures you haven't thought of for years. Old glassware? Arrange a number of pieces together to show them off. Old evening bags? A beaded bag above a doorframe or in a shadow box looks as though you hired a decorator! All those teddy bears you've collected over the years (or gathered from your child's discard pile)? Put them all in a corner and enjoy them all over again. Look with new eyes for things you can use to decorate your home.

By reviving old favorites or treasures that remind you of your child's earlier years, you create a home rich with visible memories. You will feel warm and cozy in a home that reflects your family's legacy of love.

Simple Pleasures

- Think and pray over the ways God is giving you a makeover this year.
- Journal about God's transforming touch in your life.
- Go for a hike and feel your body work hard. Thank God for mobility.

Wisdom for Living

O God, it is amazing how something as simple as a child's bowl or a grandmother's quilt can add depth and meaning to the feel of a room. Thank You for the joy and privilege of making my house a home.

When in Doubt, Use It

Now you have been pleased to bless the house of your servant, that it may continue forever in your sight; for you, O LORD, have blessed it, and it will be blessed forever.

1 CHRONICLES 17:27

Paint your house *orange?* Well, maybe not. Most of us aren't in any danger of extremes when it comes to decorating. So take some risks. Have fun with it. It is doubtful you will do anything that cannot be redone later if you change your mind.

Try something a little unexpected! An oversized picture, a shelf hung lower than usual, a red pillow in a green room. It will do wonders for your décor and for the sense of inspiration in your home.

One way to take a risk is to involve the children. Get them involved in changing the décor of their rooms or even the family room. What arrangement would they want the photos or framed art in? This is a great way to spend an afternoon or weekend with your kids.

And by all means, mix styles, colors, and textures. Change can be visually exciting. Just have a common element, such as color or design, to tie everything together. Try to get rid of preconceived notions about what you "ought" to have in a room. Think instead about what you need. I say, "When in doubt, use it!"

Simple Pleasures

- If a painting or print has been in the same spot for more than two years, move it!
- Add a footstool or ottoman and turn a rarely used corner chair into a place of leisure.
- Move rugs around the house and feel the shift in color and mood.

Wisdom for Living

You, Lord, are full of surprises! Blessings and joy abound when I live my days for You. Let me give myself over to the joy of simple surprises. A change of pace. Taking a chance.

Housework Is a Nuisance

> *The sluggard craves and gets nothing, but the desires of the diligent are fully satisfied.*
>
> PROVERBS 13:4

There's no question—housework is a nuisance! Shout it out loud. Accept the truth. Now make it better. Let's look at ways to make this nuisance a little easier, a little gentler, and a little less bothersome in our lives. I have some ideas that just might help.

Be sure to use the "Speedy Easy Method." Put on some music with a very fast beat. Cleaning will go faster—and the music will take your mind off the drudgery. Do you listen to a favorite Christian radio program? Plan a cleaning activity to do while you are listening to this. It will make the time go by fast because your mind will be focused on the topic of the day.

Here's a tip: Use your blow-dryer to blow off dust from silk flowers. Or after wiping clean your wastebaskets, give the inside bottom a coat of floor wax. It will prevent trash from sticking. Having proper tools sure helps. And don't feel everything has to be done in one session.Then, of course, there's the "Emilie Rule." Reward yourself! And when you're finished, pick some flowers for your beautiful, clean house.

Simple Pleasures

* Plan a day to go on strike. Let the kids experience the fun of doing things for themselves.
* Schedule one day a week to do a thorough cleaning for each room. Tidy up on other days.
* Cook dinner during the day and then reheat the meal when it is time. So simple!

Wisdom for Living

In everything I do, Lord, may You find the spirit of obedience, discipline, and joy—even in housework!

Welcome Home

I will bless her with abundant provisions; her poor will I satisfy with food.

PSALM 132:15

I want my life to exude an atmosphere of joy and blessing and belonging that embraces people and draws them in. I want them to feel loved and cared for! When do you feel most loved? How do you share that kind of warmth with your family, with friends, with strangers?

I truly believe we all need a place to unwind and regroup so that we can reach out and share with others what God has given us. Sound impossible? It doesn't take a lot of money or even a lot of time. What it does require is a caring and willing spirit—and determination to make room in our lives and schedules and budgets.

Opening our homes is a blessing to people. Opening our hearts to people can change lives. Find a way to express a spirit of "welcome" to someone today. A genuine smile. An offer of help. A quick prayer for someone's mentioned concern.

I hope these simple thoughts will inspire you and motivate you to encourage and nurture a spirit of welcome in your life.

Simple Pleasures

- Extend your blessings with others. Let them see the joy that only God can give.
- Share a smile with someone. You will brighten their day.
- Delight in your children's accomplishments. Share in their joy.

Wisdom for Living

*Lord, please remind me that when I welcome someone with my life,
I am welcoming them to the heart of God. May I always
keep that invitation open to people I encounter.*

Fun and Games

From the fruit of his lips a man is filled with good things as surely as the work of his hands rewards him.

As a mom and now a grandmother, I'm happy to pass along some tips for teaching children responsibility. Believe me, these ideas will also make your life a bit easier. Don't be afraid to begin teaching even your littlest child how to help out.

Make a place mat out of paper and draw the shapes of the fork, plate, spoon, and glass. Your child gets to put each item in its proper place. Or give them a pillowcase to pick up toys, trash, and papers around the house and even the yard. Help your child dress independently. If you buy coordinates, any top will go with any bottom. Or in the closet you can hang up one pair of pants followed by the shirts that match. That way they not only know what matches what, but they can help you put the clothes away after laundry.

When they're ready to put away toys, have boxes, bins, or low shelves for them to use. And don't forget to let them do it their way—arranged by them and not you. While this can be a tough one, it really does help children develop a system that makes sense to them. If they create the method, they will remember it and more likely follow it. In other words, make chores fun and games!

Simple Pleasures

- Put cookies in the oven and have your children clean their rooms until the timer goes off.
- Walk your children through some basic tasks. Do this until they can do them with confidence.
- While your child naps, take a magazine and sit in her room with her. Such sweet quiet.

Wisdom for Living

I want to pass along the goodness of hard work, Lord.
Help me have a servant's heart as I teach my child responsibility.

Have a Celebration

There, in the presence of the LORD your God, you and your families shall eat and shall rejoice in everything you have put your hand to, because the LORD your God has blessed you.

DEUTERONOMY 12:7

Today calls for a celebration. Why? Why not! You have worked hard, your family will all be together, surely there is something to rejoice over. I figure, why have just a meal when you can invest a little more and have a celebration?

By this I don't mean more money. I mean a little more thought, a little more caring. Maybe a little more time or energy, but the simpler the better. A celebration is a conscious commitment to joy. The motto in our home is: "Have card table, will travel!" Bob and I have set up love feasts in our bedroom or on the patio for just the two of us. Or set up the table in a room you don't usually eat in...the living room maybe, with a fire going. Then when dinner is cleared, you have a table all set up for a game night. We've arranged tables on the lawn to entertain big gatherings of friends and family. Sometimes our meals travel in "love baskets" packed with candles, flowers, and beautiful china.

Plan a celebration, but don't spend a lot of time on it. Just give a typical meal a bit of a twist and serve it with a heart of joy and thankfulness. If mealtime is sometimes a difficult time for you and your children, shaking up the routine might lend itself to a whole new outlook. Give God the glory for your family and friends and His faithfulness in your life.

Simple Pleasures

- Have a backwards meal. Pancakes for dinner or ravioli for breakfast!
- Let your child play their favorite music while they set the table.
- Did you forget a friend's birthday? Send her a card and a coupon for coffee.

Wisdom for Living

Dear Father, I celebrate my family. I trust in You and Your provision. And I rejoice in the breaking of bread with those I love most.

It's My Room

Whoever humbles himself like this child is the greatest in the kingdom of heaven.

MATTHEW 18:1

A day spent thinking like a child is a good day, indeed. So step out of your adult notions and restrictions and start decorating your child's bedroom.

A child's room is where you can let loose and express some of your most creative fantasies. Start with the child. Even a two-year-old can pick a favorite color or pattern when given some limited choices. Stencil names or color stripes on the wall—let your imagination have a heyday! Incorporate your child's favorite books or games or sports into the theme of the room, but don't feel that everything has to be coordinated. Remember, you are thinking like a child. So let one wall be a different color. Let the coat rack become a place to hang stuffed animals.

Paint the back of the door with blackboard paint. Or simply stretch rolls of white paper over a wall for mural-making moments. Work together with your child. Take the lead to carry out the work, but let the child really invest himself in the project as well. This will be a memory you both will enjoy for years to come.

Simple Pleasures

- Give your child's room the feel of a clubhouse, hideout, or cabin.
- Use the ceiling as a great visual space in a child's room.
- Have pictures of the family by your child's bed. It will help him feel secure.

Wisdom for Living

How I long to have the faith of a child, Lord.
Let me learn from my child. Thank You for the chance
to let my guard down and enjoy some time of pure joy.

Take Stock of Your Friends

Nevertheless, I will bring health and healing to it; I will heal my people and will let them enjoy abundant peace and security.

JEREMIAH 33:6

Why have you chosen the people who are closest to you? Let's talk about those friends of yours. Friendships keep us sane, fill many needs, and remind us of what we love so much about life.

I encourage you to think about how you respond when you're around certain people. Do you respect them? Do they encourage you to grow? Do you have a kindred spirit? Do you share like values? If the answer is yes, then you probably feel the support of this network of people in a big way. God has blessed you with a circle of friendship. But if you can't answer yes, you might want to review how much time you spend with these people. It doesn't mean the friendship is not important, but be sure that the friendship is mutual and is a positive experience for both of you. It's really a matter of "keeping it simple" in every area of life. You have a limited amount of time to spend with others, so select wisely. Much of who you are will be formed by the friends you keep. What's that old saying, "Birds of a feather flock together?"

Think about how your friends give you health and healing through their prayers and their support of who you are. What a blessing.

Simple Pleasures

Friendship, like the immortality of the soul,
is too good to believe!

—RALPH WALDO EMERSON

Wisdom for Living

*You bring people my way, Lord. I appreciate the close friends I have
and pray for those women I do not know but whom I will
someday get to know. Let my love for You always shine.
Let it never be hidden when in the presence of friends.*

Your Treasure Trove

May you be blessed for your good judgment.

1 Samuel 25:33

Our timeless treasures signal what we value most in our lives. What do you value most? Love, joy, beauty, hope, family? Treasures can be meaningful items as well as jewels of the heart. Surround yourself with both, and you will be a happy woman.

A delicate cut-glass vase, a set of antique tools, a child's drawing—any of these can be a timeless treasure. They remind us of those most cherished relationships and memories. I hope you'll take some time this summer to dig through your storage boxes, flip through photo albums, and pick up items one by one to share with your children. Tell them the stories important to your life.

Introduce your children to people who were a part of your life as a girl. This is their legacy, and it can only be passed on by you. Do your children know how you came to know the Lord? Your timeless treasures represent your heritage of love and memory. They tell your story…a story definitely worth telling. Keep them close to your heart, and then pass them on. Your children will be blessed by this time with you and with their family history. And if your child has not yet made a decision of faith, hearing your personal story will encourage them and make them more comfortable to ask questions.

You see, there are many kinds of treasures to protect and pass along to those you love. Don't miss any of them!

Simple Pleasures

- Start recording your child's story with a journal or record book.
- Write essays about things you remember as a girl.
- Fill your garden with flowers you recall from your mother's garden.

Wisdom for Living

God, You provide me with so many treasures. I will take care of them.
Share them. And offer them back to You.

Saving Money

You will have plenty to eat, until you are full, and you will praise the name of the LORD your God, who has worked wonders for you.

JOEL 2:26

The best way to save money when you hit the supermarket is to plan ahead. Check your local newspaper ads for sales. If something is on sale, buy in quantity. Generic brands can be a savings. By all means avoid impulse buying. Studies estimate that nearly 50 percent of all purchases are unplanned. Good for the store, bad for you! Complete your shopping in half an hour. It's those extra minutes that bring on the impulse buying. "Who cares?" Well, for one, I do! You know why? Because it gives me more hours in my day—and more money in my pocket—to do those things that count the most.

I am sure that you can think of a few things right away that you would rather do than grocery shop. And if you cannot, then you definitely need to include some leisure time in your life. There is only one you. Give *you* a break by planning ahead on the shopping. Then check that task off your list and move on to something fun. Is life about being a great shopper? No, it's about being the woman God has for you to be—and that takes some leisure time.

Simple Pleasures

- Clip your coupons the weekend before you go shopping. Take only the ones you want.
- Promise yourself some down time after you go to the grocery store.
- Simplify your family's food selection. Go for the basics and add spices for variety.

Wisdom for Living

Time for life. Time for You. Time to fall in love with the blessings in my life. That is what I will make room for today, Lord.

Sacrifice thank offerings to God,
fulfill your vows to the Most High.

PSALM 50:14

I wouldn't be Emilie Barnes if I didn't encourage you to plan a tea party! You already know that I believe a tea party is a marvelous way to nurture relationships with your women friends. But if tea parties are not yet a part of your life, let me give you some simple ways to have one and some easy opportunities to introduce the idea to new and old friends.

Invite them for a Saturday morning teatime brunch. Or have tea, watch old movies, and work on a project together. A tea does not have to be just a group of women sitting around the living room all day sipping out of china cups. Have a tea in the garden and then ask your friends to help you plant flowers. It won't take long and what a joy it will be when you host a second tea to celebrate the beautiful blooms you planted.

Or get a group of your friends together for a spa day. Have the staff serve tea (they usually do anyway) or take along some of your special cups and saucers and use those. What a way to enjoy a manicure or a pedicure. Tea parties have become all the rage—have you noticed? Be creative. Think about what you like and how you enjoy expressing yourself. Then send out those invitations. You'll be so glad you did!

Simple Pleasures

- Visit a nursing home and ask to visit people who do not have any family.
- Host a tea for a new bride or new mother.
- Have a thank-you tea for school teachers or Sunday school teachers.

Wisdom for Living

Lord, I love my friends and am strengthened by their presence
and their support. I will pray for each woman I plan to invite to tea.
Let this be a part of my ministry.

The Annual Garage Sale

Give to him as the LORD your God has blessed you.

DEUTERONOMY 15:14

Summer is just about over, so isn't it about time for the annual garage sale? If you have school-age children at home, what better way to clean out the garage, closets, and storage areas? Go through all that stuff and decide what you want to sell and how much it's going to go for. Display the items in categories. Use picnic tables and card tables to display breakable items. And never underestimate what will sell. The old popcorn popper, iron, clock. Get up early and commit the day to your sale. Plan something fun, like a barbecue, for when it's over. If you have a child old enough to use the barbecue, sell hot dogs off the grill for a quarter to bring in the customers and give your sale a festive feel. Younger children can set up a lemonade stand and get involved too.

Really find ways to clean out the cluttered places of your home. Enter the new season with less stuff and more space. Maybe the money can be used for children's back-to-school clothing or materials.

And here's an idea. Commit a part—or even all—of your sales to a missionary project at your church. Make it a worthwhile end of summertime for the entire family!

Simple Pleasures

- Give yourself ten minutes in each room to gather "stuff." This first round will make you want to go back and look again.
- Create a garage sale box and add to it as you come across items to sell. Keep price stickers in the box for quick pricing. You will be ready for your next garage sale.
- Ask others to join in for added fun and stuff to sell.

Wisdom for Living

O God, remove from my pathway anything that hinders my faith.
Let me never rely on the things in my life. May I always
have a heart that is willing to part with stuff!

I'm Exhausted

Those who hope in the LORD will renew their strength. They will soar on wings like eagles; they will run and not grow weary, they will walk and not be faint.

ISAIAH 40:31

The thought of "everything I didn't do yesterday...added to everything I haven't done today...plus everything I won't do tomorrow...completely exhausts me!" Don't think about this, it will overwhelm you. Instead, let's do something about your situation before it all adds up to a life of stress.

I realized a long time ago that if women could adopt simple ideas and methods, they would have more hours in their day. Time management is personal. But getting the most out of life is a universal desire. We all have 24 hours in a day and 365 days in a year. Are you making them count? Set some goals. Plan them and work them! This, of course, is the key. The doing part. Maybe you have a friend who shares your desire to organize her time better. You could meet once a week to plan next week's schedules. This way you are held accountable for at least doing the planning. Yes, I am saying you could plan your planning. Why not? As long as you keep it simple and manageable.

You'll soon discover you have more time to do the things you really want to do. More time to spend on projects, career, family, and spiritual growth. Only you know what you are willing to try and take on right now. Maybe it is a bad time for a big life change. Start with basic planning. Schedule the big stuff and the anchor spiritual growth times, like morning devotions, and go from there. You'll have more time to simply become the woman that God wants you to be. It is a great joy.

Simple Pleasures

- Have a no-television evening for the whole family.
- Plan a trip to take some day. List the stops you'd like to make.
- Sign up for a workout class or a swim fitness class.

Wisdom for Living

Whom do You desire for me to be, Lord?
Help me take the time to find that out.

Glory in his holy name; let the hearts of those who seek the LORD rejoice. Look to the LORD and his strength; seek his face always.

PSALM 105:3-4

If you spend time alone with God in the morning, you'll start your day refreshed and ready for whatever comes your way. God works better than your morning coffee, the one thing you may imagine you cannot start the day without. Now how much more important is God than a latte? Need I say more?

And if you spend time alone with God in the evening, you'll go to sleep relaxed and resting in His care. You'll be ready for a new day to serve Him. I can't speak for you, but I need a touch of God's love, joy, peace, patience, kindness, goodness, faithfulness, gentleness, and self-control every day of my life. Those are exactly the things God wants to give us as His children, along with guidance, wisdom, hope, grace, and a deeper knowledge of Him.

Decide when you would like to spend that time with God. Say it out loud, kind of like inviting a friend over for that morning coffee. You will enjoy the idea of meeting God for a personal talk. It will become a highlight of the day, and you will thirst for more.

Listen to these wise words: "Every little glimpse that can be gained of God…exceeds every pain…every joy…that man or woman can conceive." Bless you today—simply and wonderfully!

Simple Pleasures

- Color outside of the lines in all that you do today.
- Before you get upset about something your child has done, ask yourself if it is important.
- Pray with a child who is angry. It will soften her heart.

Wisdom for Living

God, let's plan a date. Here and now. I will meet You at my kitchen table at _____. I cannot wait to share my life with You every day.

Children!

He who fears the LORD has a secure fortress, and for his children it will be a refuge.

PROVERBS 14:26

As a mom you are probably saying, "When will school begin again?" I suggest taking a practical approach to your children's presence around the house. I have some simple tips for getting them to help out.

It is amazing how plastic bins, pegs, hampers, baskets, and hooks give your children resources to pick up and put away their things. Here's an idea for young children when they want a straw for their drink. Cut it off short so it's easier to hold and drink from and they can do it themselves. Put a laundry basket in each child's room. Then on laundry day, have everyone sort their pile at one time. See who has the most whites, darks, stripes, and so on.

Give a child a dry dust mop and let him swoosh around the hardwood floors. He will actually get most of the dust! When the lawn furniture is dirty, give young children a cup of water and a small paint brush. While they pretend to paint a chair, they are cleaning it.

Another important tip: Catch a child doing something good and tell him or her about it. Be positive and uplifting. And when all else fails, get a friend to come over and give you a break! You deserve it. In fact, I think you should try to regularly schedule these breaks. You need to keep up with your interests, friends, and moments of solitude so that you stay content and grounded.

Simple Pleasures

- Have your children write down goals for the rest of the summer.
- Create a reading competition for your children. See who can read the most books.
- Walk tall, with good posture. You will feel good and look great.

Wisdom for Living

Father, even when things get a little crazy, don't let me wish away one moment of my day or my time with my children. They truly are precious to me.

Be Selfish at Times

Be at rest once more, O my soul, for the LORD has been good to you.

PSALM 116:7

I want to give you permission to be selfish sometimes. Yes, you read that right. I know your heart grows heavy under the strain of being a mother. You feel the fatigue in your bones, don't you? A lack of sleep and attention to your needs will build over time and become too heavy for you to carry.

When I was a young mom, I was exhausted most days. All I wanted to do was take a hot bath and slip into bed for a really long time. After several years of that, I said, "I need help!" One of the things I did was to get up a half hour before everyone else. It gave me a chance to spend time in my Bible over an early cup of tea. I can't tell you the impact this time alone with God had on my outlook. As I've matured, I've discovered that I am a better parent and wife when I have time for myself. And you know what? I soon realized I had plenty left over to share with my loved ones. A little time alone before the Lord is a simple thing with profound results!

If this is hard for you to do, it probably means you also have a hard time giving your burdens over to God. Learn to ask for help. It is not a sign of weakness or failure, but of strength, courage, and health.

Simple Pleasures

* Pray to God today and offer Him the burdens that occupy your mind.
* Ask your children what they worry about. Give them comfort and assurance.
* Be a source of help for another mother this week. Maybe she has a hard time asking.

Wisdom for Living

Help! Help! Help! Lord, it feels so good to place my worries at Your feet. I am tired. Give me strength. I am discouraged. Give me a hopeful heart.

Take Hectic Out of the Day

My soul is weary with sorrow; strengthen me according to your word.

PSALM 119:28

Moms with children of all ages understand what "hectic" means. How often are you juggling schedules and people while calculating where you should be next and what you will need when you get there?

I have found that getting myself organized is the key to having time for the things God wants me to do with my life. Now I am not talking about perfection! But simplifying a few daily activities that have grown to become big parts of your day can make all the difference.

Here are some simple ideas. Use a kitchen silverware tray to store art supplies, children's crayons, and pencils. Colored plastic rings are great for color-coding your keys. Whenever you add a new item, discard an old one. By the way, leave some slack in your day for surprises, interruptions, and emergencies. Some things take longer no matter how carefully you plan. One of the secrets of success is to enjoy doing whatever you do, not only for yourself, but also for the satisfaction of giving to others.

Simple Pleasures

- Keep a box of granola bars in the car so the children can snack while you run errands.
- Substitute water for soda and other sugary drinks. You'll have more energy.
- Teach your children to set the table. This will help with mealtime preparation.

Wisdom for Living

Lord, where do I need to save time and where do I need to spend time? Guide me to always be a good and faithful steward of my time.

Living Alfresco

> I will refresh the weary and satisfy the faint.
>
> JEREMIAH 31:25

Here is a tip on how to refresh your soul—surround yourself with God's beauty every chance you get. Bring the outdoors in and live in the outdoors whenever possible. Delight in nature as fully as you can.

If you're lucky enough to have a room with a lot of morning sunshine, turn it into a sunroom. Decorate with wicker or outdoor furniture, and add plenty of comfortable cushions and houseplants everywhere. Fresh flowers are the best way I know to bring the outdoors in. And don't worry too much about elaborate arrangements. Keep the effect simple and fresh. Old windows make wonderful lawn and garden decorations. We once had one hanging by chains from a wall of our patio.

Plan ways to enjoy experiences outdoors. Plan a large outdoor meal and invite friends, family, and neighbors over to celebrate the beginning or end of a season. Have your dinner prayer be focused on rejoicing in God's bounty, and let it be a time of real thanksgiving.

While the weather is nice, throw open the windows and enjoy the warmth of the sunshine! Ah—the simple pleasures of life!

Simple Pleasures

- Install a simple, small fountain in your backyard. It will soothe your mind and soul.
- Take your evening tea or iced tea outside tonight. Watch the twilight dance.
- Serve a big pasta meal outdoors for friends and family. Celebrate each other.

Wisdom for Living

Your bounty surrounds me, Lord.
It fills me with joy and with deep thanksgiving.

Who Has That Kind of Time?

Teach us to make the most of our time, so that we may grow in wisdom.

PSALM 90:12 NLT

If you were offered more time or more money at this very moment, which would you take? Most busy moms want the time. Time for themselves. Time for their spouse and family. Time to think about how they would use extra time if they ever had any.

Time can feel like a mother's worst enemy. But if you start incorporating just a few time-saving habits every other month, soon you will have a more organized, user-friendly approach to your life. Wouldn't you rather spend a few moments in stillness, rest, and catching your breath instead of throwing time away on a redundant task?

Do you ever have time to read all the magazines you receive? Why not clip out the articles that look interesting and file them away for later? Sort your mail as soon as you receive it. Place bills in a special folder, and recycle ads, junk mail, and opened envelopes to avoid clutter. Keep track of gift giving with a monthly planner so that you don't waste time and money on a last-minute gift-buying spree. Add sizes and color preferences for future giving. Have a secret shelf for gifts. When you find something on sale, "wrap and tag" it for future giving. Don't forget to buy spare blank all-occasion cards too. The goal is to take care of basic tasks while it is time-efficient, rather than when it is inconvenient.

Simple Pleasures

* Give yourself time and room to breathe today.
* Notice when you tense up. Take a moment to stretch upwards.
* Sit on the floor, lean against a wall, and read a book the way you did when you were a kid.

Wisdom for Living

*Father, my time is Yours. Help me to spend it wisely always.
May I make room for the priorities and blessings
You fill my life with each day.*

September

YOU ARE MY SANCTUARY

The Gift of Every Day

*May the LORD make you increase,
both you and your children. May
you be blessed by the LORD, the
Maker of heaven and earth.*

PSALM 115:14

I love my teacups, my quilts, my family photos, my letters, and my albums. But they are still just things—and things are not what matter in the long run.

Let's face it, most of our possessions will eventually be lost, cracked, or broken. But the time you and I invest today in our families, friends, and in keeping close to our Savior will never be wasted or lost. Why is it that trivial activities and obligations sometimes seem more pressing and more important than the simple act of spending time with our families? Talking, laughing, playing, praying, and just being together. Don't let the world direct you toward false treasures. Home is where the heart is! So make it so. Don't let a day go by without embracing this truth. .

The time and energy you invest in loving others—that's timeless! It will shape memories that shape souls. This is what gives your legacy its meaning. And every day, every moment does count toward eternity. It's the love you give now that will make them want to keep your photo on the wall.

Simple Pleasures

* Think about how you want to use your home to show your heart this week.
* Help your kids plan a slumber party. Plan for lots of laughter and fatigue!
* Ask your children how they might like to use their home to care for others.

Wisdom for Living

Make my life a treasure hunt, Lord. Where will I discover my heart today? Where will I see Your heart unfold in my activities today?

Looking for a Masterpiece

Restore us, O God; make your face shine upon us, that we may be saved.

PSALM 80:3

Masterpieces can come in all kinds of packaging. And as far as I'm concerned, the best finds are those that cost absolutely nothing. That's what you may come across in your mother's attic, your neighbor's garage, or a friend's back porch. If you see something you think you can use, it never hurts to ask if you can have it, buy it, or swap it. Garage sales, swap meets, flea markets, and estate sales are great sources of decorating bargains. Junk shops—I spell that j-u-n-q-u-e!—are also wonderful places to find treasures for your home. Just make sure you know what you like and stick to your budget and needs.

If you have young kids, you can use this idea and create your own swap meet. Think of the many toys and slightly chewed board books that fill your closets and shelves. Arrange a play date and have each mom bring along five used, age-appropriate items for exchange. The kids get "new" playthings without adding to the ever-growing toy box.

The idea is to simplify the home environment. Less clutter and a consistent style will add peace to the home front.

Simple Pleasures

- Light a candle while your children eat breakfast. See how it sets a new morning mood.
- Do a prayer walk through your house. Pray for your family in each room.
- Take a magazine to a local park and enjoy sitting outside.

Wisdom for Living

Lord, thank You for transforming the brokenness of my life ·into a perfect, whole vessel. May I always look beyond the cracks and smudges of everything and everyone to find the masterpiece within.

Cozy Areas

My people will live in peaceful dwellling places, in secure homes, in undisturbed places of rest.

ISAIAH 32:18

Where do you go for a place of sanctuary within your home? Do you have a favorite corner where you snuggle with a quilt and a good book? Where in your house does everyone like to gather? Where do you invite your guests to sit for conversation?

Whatever room or space comes to mind, this area should be comfortable as well as beautiful...even impressive! It's truly the heart of your home. You want to make sure you have comfortable seating, whether it's a couch and chairs or mismatched rocking chairs circling your fireplace. You want something that beckons people to draw close to one another. Use your decorating savvy to make it cute. Use slipcovers in gorgeous fabrics, pillows, perhaps a fuzzy throw. Use your paintbrush and fabric to dress up inexpensive director's chairs. Why bother? Because it says to another person, "I care about you!"

A home is a refuge from the busyness of life, work, carpools, and crazy schedules. With a little effort, you can transform a corner into a warm nest just right for hugging your kids and talking about the day. Or an unused hallway corner becomes a soothing place to read in the sunshine. Let places of rest and relaxation bless you and your family and guests.

Simple Pleasures

- Look at a photo album and reflect on good memories with your loved ones.
- Enjoy God's creatures. Spend time playing with kittens or puppies.
- Listen to your children playing and give thanks for their happiness and well-being.

Wisdom for Living

Father, help me to see ways to add peace and tranquility to an area.
Let simple ideas create a place of community and a refuge
where I can sit and talk with You.

Being Blessed

> *I will bless them and the places surrounding my hill. I will send down showers in season; there will be showers of blessing.*
>
> EZEKIEL 34:26

If you're like most of the women I know, you want a life that reflects your personality and renews your soul. But how do you go about it when much of your life is spent tending to the needs of others? I know it isn't always easy, but it can be simple.

Numbers 6:24 says: "The LORD bless you and keep you; the LORD make his face shine upon you and be gracious to you; the LORD turn his face toward you and give you peace." What a wonderful sentiment to hand-letter and hang by your front door! It will speak to you, your family, and your guests! To further express your personality, have a potluck "chez vous." Invite guests to bring something that suits the theme you have chosen. Or start a supper club and meet in different homes each month with a unique menu. Use the season as your inspiration. In winter, cut out paper snowflakes to use as place markers. Potted flowers add color and warmth to a spring dinner gathering. Summer is the perfect time to use seashells to decorate the table. Sprinkle glitter around them as decorative homemade sand. In fall, go to a local farm, pick pumpkins, and use them for centerpieces, yard decorations, and, of course, pumpkin pie!

These simple efforts remind us of what is worthwhile. The smiles of family and friends reflect the Lord's face shining on you.

Simple Pleasures

Everyone has inside of him a piece of good news. The good news is that you don't know how great you can be! How much you can love!
—ANNE FRANK

Wisdom for Living

*Lord, the simple treasures of Your natural world bring me peace
in every season of the year. Thank You for the pleasures
that remind me I am unique and precious in Your sight.*

The Nicest Word

May there be peace within your walls and security within your citadels.

PSALM 122:7

"There's no place like home." I agree. Don't you love that phrase: "at home"? What does it bring to your mind? Do you think of the people who encourage you and love you, or do you recall childhood memories of your first bedroom or the first time you helped make dinner?

To me it says so much about being cozy in my own nest. About being where I belong. About tending to the most important areas of my life. The world may be whizzing by outside—but here I'm safe, peaceful. My favorite days are the ones I spend here with my husband when our children and grandchildren are all over the place. And I love to welcome other people in and make them feel comfortable and loved. One of my favorite phrases is, "Come on in!" And you know what? That's exactly what God is saying to you today. "Come on in! I'm here for all of you who labor and are in need of rest. I'm welcoming you with open arms."

I pray that home also brings to mind a sense of love and peace. Because this is what God intended home to be. There are days when I wonder exactly what our heavenly home will be like. It fills me with joy to think about the welcome we will receive from our Savior! This feeling of joy is what you bring to your own home. As you nurture love and kindness for your family, you are defining home for them.

Simple Pleasures

- Play Scrabble with your family.
- Start a big crossword puzzle.
- Watch the *Wizard of Oz* and be grateful for your home.

Wisdom for Living

Dear Lord, help me to mirror the love of heaven
within my home. Let all who enter my doors feel like
family. And may I be reminded that my heart
has a precious home in Your grace.

Ideas for Comfortable Kitchens

Let them come to me for refuge;
let them make peace with me, yes,
let them make peace with me.

ISAIAH 27:5

When I think of the word "cozy," I think of a lovely kitchen on a cool autumn day. Checkered drapes are open and the view outside of falling yellow leaves and the first gentle rain magnify the security and warmth on the inside. The kitchen can, in every season, host the best seat in the house with a few special touches.

Light a candle! Place it on a windowsill, and you'll see your kitchen in an entirely new light! Pretty cotton dish towels make beautiful napkins, place mats, or even cafe curtains. If you have a large kitchen, add a rocking chair or an upholstered chair with a footstool. Store foods in ways that allow them to be decorative as well as useful. Keep your olive oil and vinegar in pretty decanters. On a slow afternoon, put on soft music and browse through your recipe books for ideas. Set aside a Saturday morning. Learn how to really use one of those appliances stored in the cabinet. When you have guests, greet them with a wonderful goodie, and then put aprons on them and let them help. It works!

Let your light shine before men (and women and all your company). Creating an atmosphere of hospitality will let those who enter the heart of your house know that it is really, truly a home.

Simple Pleasures

- Spend time in your kitchen to enjoy it as a room, not as a place of work.
- Make this heart of your home a spiritual heart as well with Scriptures on the wall.
- Open the windows to the kitchen and feel the fall breeze.

Wisdom for Living

Father, when it is cold on the outside, I will look to the beauty
of the world, especially the world I have created inside my home.
Please help me to remember to be still and know that You are God.

Beautiful Private Rooms

Let all who take refuge in you be glad; let them ever sing for joy. Spread your protection over them, that those who love your name may rejoice in you.

Intimate spaces and intimate relationships have a lot in common. Creating small, personal spaces within your home will encourage moments of rest, devotion, and peace.

Do your private rooms—the bedroom and bathroom—welcome you? Have you spent the same effort for the "retreat places" as you have for where you welcome guests? Keep a journal and your Bible on your bedside table. It encourages intimacy with God. Have a blend of candles or potpourri in bedside and bathroom drawers to fill the room with subtle scents everytime you search for an item.

For wonderful ideas about decorating a bedroom or bath, browse through department stores or gift shops. Go ahead—adapt and copy! Use colorful sheets to make pillows, wall coverings, and comforter covers. And, of course, you can use them as sheets too! Garland a large picture with a swag of greenery or flowers. But don't restrict your restful or romantic touches to the bed and bath—just start there! Your home is not just a shelter from the elements, it is a place of shelter from the busy pace outside your front door. Create a sanctuary and seek solitude in these beautiful personal spaces.

Simple Pleasures

- Set ground rules so children, even little ones, respect the privacy of others.
- Give your children a special place to pray in their room.
- Buy a new shower curtain for a quick but significant face-lift.

Wisdom for Living

I want to seek solace and comfort in my home, Lord.
I want a place to calm my spirit and to experience renewal.
Help me make my home that place.

Starting with You

"Me—get organized?" Yes, you! I can almost guarantee that when you start a few organizational projects you will get excited about simplifying an area of your life. Getting organized is pretty simple, but it has to start with you! And I think it has to start with baby steps.

Have you noticed? Organized people have a calmness about them that disorganized people don't have. What's causing all the confusion? You're going to have to get rid of the clutter in your life before you can move on. First of all, make sure everything has a place. If there's no place for stuff to go, it's going to get piled. Get rid of all items you don't use. And start involving the entire family. This is a big key to making organization an ongoing family trait. Learn to delegate jobs to your kids. Keep lists! I have them everywhere. If you're going to have time for the important things, more organization is key.

Be encouraged—it gets easier once you get started! Trust me. Life can be a lot simpler. And when you put organization into practice, it leads to a more balanced life. You and your family will reap the benefits.

Simple Pleasures

- Program phone numbers in your home phone and cell phone and write them in your planner.
- On the weekend, organize your outfits for the upcoming week.
- Create a checklist for camping trips so you don't forget something important.

Wisdom for Living

Where do I start, Lord? Sometimes I feel so scattered.
Help me learn to help myself and my family by creating
a lifestyle that is peaceful and calm. I cannot wait.

189

Plants and Flowers

Then have them make a sanctuary for me, and I will dwell among them.

EXODUS 25:8

Nature is such a source of inspiration. Look around you! Then find a way to bring it indoors and into your life. Use flowers and plants to decorate your home. A brass pot of zinnias on the coffee table that picks up the print in your curtains will do wonders in your living room. And the dark corner of your family room will come alive if you brighten it with a container of philodendron. Your entryway is the perfect spot for a bowl of geraniums or freshly picked roses. How about the fireplace in the summertime? Use a pleated paper fan spread across the opening, or fill it with flowers or candles.

Consider the colors of nature as your home's palette. A warm touch of olive green with a hint of autumn red or gold in a room will bring the soothing feel of your yard to your indoor experience. Or splash walls with stripes of sunshine yellow and cool water blue.

Use your creativity to make your home a beautiful place—a place where there's a comfortable spot to open your Bible and spend some time reading, studying, and praying. It keeps life a lot more simple.

Simple Pleasures

- Buy small watering cans for the children. Let them be a part of nurturing plant life.
- Set up a swing in the backyard, one for children and adults to enjoy.
- Think of your yard as another room. Fill it with love, beauty, and activity.

Wisdom for Living

Your creation inspires me, Lord. It also shows me who You are. You are a Lord that cares about beauty and about the smallest of treasures.

It's Time to Get Quiet

The LORD gives strength to his people; the LORD blesses his people with peace.

PSALM 29:11

I don't know about you, but a little stillness is always good for my soul. It helps to keep life just a bit simpler.

Don't be afraid to take time out when things get to be too much. If you don't have small children, set a timer for 15 minutes and disappear into your bedroom. If you do have small children, arrange for a friend or neighbor to sit with your children for an hour every couple of weeks.

Read your Bible—or simply lie still and do nothing! If you work outside the home, set aside your lunch hour as a time to reconnect, a time for some stillness. Take a walk. Drive to a park. Read, pray, and return to your job refreshed. Remember, the times when you feel you can't afford to slow down—those are usually the times you need to most.

If you're squirming just thinking about this, that is a signal! It's time to get still. This is the time God can especially speak to your heart. You cannot listen for His voice in the clutter of daily chatter and the noise of busyness. You know the expression, "I cannot hear myself think." Well, how true this is. Allow yourself the time and peace to listen.

Simple Pleasures

- Kneel and pray to God this morning.
- Take a long shower and use a fragrant shower gel to refresh your spirit.
- Think before you speak. It saves energy and often saves the situation.

Wisdom for Living

I seek You in the stillness of early morning, Lord. I listen for Your voice in the stillness of an afternoon moment of rest. When I pause to hear the song of a bird, I am letting myself breathe in Your peace.

Think Through the Room

Her ways are pleasant ways, and all her paths are peace.

PROVERBS 3:17

Go stand in the center of a room in your house. Really! This is a fun exercise. There you are in the middle of a room, wondering what to do to make it look fabulous. Where do you start? I will be your décor coach. Let's go.

Okay, build from the basics—the furnishings and their arrangement. Then pretend you're a guest. What's working? What's pleasing to the eye? For example, try keeping a clear visual line from the entryway to the seating areas. Even chairs grouped around a fireplace can be angled so they appear to invite visitors over. And remember, color is one of the easiest—and most inexpensive—ways to unify a room. Try to fill in the blanks with creative accessories—pillows, baskets, and candles.

Chances are that you sometimes entertain guests with children the same age as yours. Your home is probably already child friendly for that age group, but I suggest going beyond just child friendly. Make your home child inviting. Children respond to feeling welcome too. Do you have pretty, welcoming things at their eye level?

Simple ideas can create a simply inviting home!

Simple Pleasures

- Have a fall housewarming party. Fill your home with candles and serve cider and tea.
- Change the colors in your house with simple additions like candles, tablecloths, and rugs.
- Think of a friend with a different style than you. What would she do to change a room?

Wisdom for Living

Who will enter my home needing comfort, Lord?
Who needs a place of welcome and refuge?
Let me see clearly how I can invite them in to Your love.

Chore Charts

Train a child in the way he should go, and when he is old he will not turn from it.

PROVERBS 22:6

You need help around the house. And your children need to learn responsibility. Aha! If you don't already have a system in place for making this happen, you might want to consider a "Chore Chart" for your children.

A "Chore Chart" can help your kids perceive their worth and value to the family. Even at two and three years of age, children can begin to be responsible for some areas in the home—personal hygiene, dusting their furniture, picking up their clothes, helping set the table. For the little ones, the chart can have simple pictures that can be checked off as the chore is completed. Whatever the ages, children need a checklist to show them how they're doing. You can also come up with some sort of reward system. But let the feeling of accomplishment be the biggest reward. Just like you, a child receives satisfaction by completing tasks and having that achievement noted.

Daily you will be building up your children and preparing them for bigger decisions and responsibilities as they grow older. Sharing in the work becomes a way of life and a way that children enjoy being a part of a family.

Simple Pleasures

- Prepare your children to be good decision makers. Let them have responsibility.
- Encourage a young child so that they will be eager to take on more as they get older.
- Model for your older children how to help the younger ones. Teamwork works!

Wisdom for Living

O God, encouraging the growth of my child is important.
Let me raise a child who shares in the work of a family.
And let them learn to see this as a labor of love.

Decorating Magic

Blessed is the man who finds wisdom, the man who gains understanding, for she is more profitable than silver and yields better returns than gold.

The secret to shopping without blowing your budget is finding gold in the least likely places! Just think, every time you don't spend money, you are saving money!

I have a few simple ideas for inexpensive decorating magic. First of all, check out your grandmother's attic or your neighbor's garage. (Be sure to get permission first!) If you see something you think you might use, it never hurts to ask if they're willing to part with it.

Garage sales, swap meets, flea markets, and estate sales are great resources for decorating gems. You can take advantage of these opportunities by having measurements of rooms or open spaces written on an index card. Make a list of items you would like to find so you can stick to priorities. If you see a pricey item at an antique store or flea market, keep checking back for a markdown and be sure to express your offer each time.

A professional decorator once told me that at least 25 percent of your furnishings and accessories should feature quality materials. A beautiful chair or an art print will balance your discount-store linens or junk-shop mirror. Old and new blend together with great grace. It's the secret to decorating beautifully on a budget!

Simple Pleasures

- Plan to meet a friend for a morning of estate sale shopping.
- Sit in an heirloom piece of furniture you own and read your morning devotion.
- Invite neighbors over for tea and use antique cups only.

Wisdom for Living

My walk with You, Lord, is one of my treasures.
It is the anchor for my life and my key to restoration.

Genie in the Glass Bottle

I will listen to what God the LORD will say; he promises peace to his people, his saints—but let them not return to folly.

PSALM 85:8

Credit cards are the "genie in the glass bottle." They let us enter into a world of make-believe. While it can be so nice to have something today that is beyond your checking account's capacity, you are actually taking away from tomorrow's financial opportunities and freedom. This includes your child's future as well.

When it comes to money, seek paths to security and freedom, not risk and restriction. You will not have the benefit of giving back to the Lord if your money is trapped into cycles of debt.

Debt will prevent you from managing your money properly. We can't be financially free as long as the monster of debt controls our lives. Pay off the balance at the end of each statement. If you're behind, stop using your card. Never purchase a large item on the same day you have the impulse to buy. Stay within your credit line, and use only one card for all expenses. And cut up your cards if you can't manage them.

Give these four secrets a try: Earn little by little. Save little by little. Share your blessings with others. And stay out of debt!

Simple Pleasures

- When you are tempted to buy with credit, think how the interest could be used for good.
- Plan ahead for small goals. See what is coming up every quarter and save accordingly.
- Schedule your cars for regular maintenance to save in the long run.

Wisdom for Living

Lord, let the use of my blessings honor You.
Let my actions be focused on stewardship today
and security for tomorrow.

Cozy and Homey

When you enter a house, first say, "Peace to this house."

LUKE 10:5

Starting your morning in God's Word surrounds you with history, stories, and the warmth of God's message for you today. This sense of legacy and memory can also be pulled from your own past, your own stories. Here are some ways to blend your home today with the celebrations and love of yesterday.

Photos and vacation souvenirs are wonderful for making your house feel like home. Make sure there's always something warm near your sofa or chair for snuggling—an heirloom afghan, a quilt, a flea market find, a vintage blanket. When you're not using it, stack it beneath a table, or simply drape it over the arm of a chair. Instead of the traditional lamp table, try wooden trunks, perhaps ones that someone in your family has used to make a long journey. An old trunk serves beautifully for both coffee table and storage. Tell stories with the elements you bring into your home and use daily. They add such a homey feel.

The idea is to be creative—to make your home the place your family wants to be! Surrounded by souvenirs of a legacy, your family today will be creating their own piece of history in your family's ongoing story.

Simple Pleasures

- Find a colorful blooming plant to spruce up your kitchen table.
- Dust with scented furniture polish to add a delightful aroma to your home.
- Put dryer softener sheets in dresser drawers for added freshness.

Wisdom for Living

Lord, You have blessed me with a resting place. A cozy refuge during the storm of life. This is my home. I carry with me the love of generations, and I want to pass it on. Help me do that, I pray.

Getting off the Phone

Set a guard over my mouth, O LORD; keep watch over the door of my lips.

PSALM 141:3

How many times have you been stuck on the phone and unable to end the conversation? Or deep in a conversation with a friend when you notice it is time to go watch your daughter play soccer? It sounds so very simple, but if you take control of the telephone and how much time it uses up, you will create more time for things that need to be done, including resting.

If you're attached to that cell phone of yours, this may not be for you! But for the rest of us, here goes. To free yourself more quickly, warn people in advance that your time is limited. Or try, "Before we hang up…" It's a reminder that your call will end soon. Turn off the phone when you don't want to be disturbed—especially during family times. It lets your children know they are a priority. And for those with cell phones, watch out for its intrusion on family times. Turn it off at a child's event or activity. When you are driving and have the child in the car, use that time to talk to them, not to anyone else. Show your family that nothing is as important as time with them.

And when you leave a message, give as much information as possible. It may eliminate another call. Excuse me…is that my phone ringing?

Simple Pleasures

- Set times when you take and make calls so that you can get your tasks done.
- Teach your children phone etiquette early on.
- Model pleasant communication for your children, and don't be on the phone long.

Wisdom for Living

*Father, remind me when I forget that conveniences
that take over life are not an asset. Control of helpful devices
will save me time and help balance life. After all, You are
the most important one to talk to, and no phone is required.*

Stress Beater

> All your sons will be taught by the LORD, and great will be your children's peace.
>
> ISAIAH 54:13

Mothers know stress very well! While at first you might feed off of stress to get things done, eventually you will burn out at a certain point. Maybe today is one of those days when you feel you are running around in circles. God wants your life to be sane. When you are scattered and tired, you are not taking care of the life He has given you. He wants more for you. And so do I. And, I imagine, so do you!

I have some ideas that can help you breathe more easily and alleviate some of that stress. The key? It's called *organization!* Don't groan. That word may sound like work, but it really leads to a better life. Here are some of the ingredients you'll need:

- a quality period of time with God each day
- a list of carefully thought through long-term and short-term goals
- monthly calendar/weekly schedule book/pad of daily schedules

Are you beginning to get the picture? If you're going to be organized, you've got to have some tools and plans to stay on course. Then mix the ingredients liberally and season them with prayer. The result will be an organized home and a more peaceful, happier woman! Are you ready to begin? Don't delay a moment longer in working toward a more organized you. Are you excited? You are going to love it!

Simple Pleasures

Drop thy still dews of quietness till all our strivings cease;
take from our souls the strain and stress, and let
our ordered lives confess the beauty of Thy peace.

—JOHN GREENLEAF WHITTIER

Wisdom for Living

*I need to get organized! I really want to be a better steward
of time for myself and my family and for You, Lord.
I want to live a life that is calmer and more fulfilling.*

My Evil Twin

Turn from evil and do good; seek peace and pursue it.

PSALM 34:14

I don't know about you, but I have this "evil twin" living inside me! This is a day of true confessions. Do you know the "evil twin" syndrome? It's that Martha/Mary thing from Luke chapter 10. My Martha side says, "Sweep, mop, clean! Don't waste a minute. Dirt is sin and I'm wallowing in it!" But my Mary side says, "Hey, housework can wait. There's a friend I must see who's lonely and needs someone right now." Martha nags me to keep my house spotless, and Mary says gently, "I need time to pray." It's the dilemma of being today's woman, isn't it? I desire to be like Mary, but my Martha side keeps getting in the way.

Don't be overrun with the guilt of this split personality. It touches all of us. It is indeed hard to find the balance. But we are called to be both. I think within each of us, one of these personalities is more dominant, wouldn't you say? Which are you on most days? When you are feeling stressed in a situation, think about whether you are being too Mary or too Martha. Chances are, shifting your perspective a little will help you bring a godly balance to the situation.

You may want to use my Martha-Mary-Me prayer: "O God, in compassion, so order my days that Mary might serve You and Martha may praise You."

Simple Pleasures

- Learn how to recognize when that twin is making an appearance.
- Balance duties and a prayerful life of stillness and reflection.
- Ask your spouse how you can help him develop his spiritual life more.

Wisdom for Living

*Lord, thank You for the example of Mary and Martha in Your Word.
What role models they are. Help me to seek balance
so that I serve You and serve others with Your blessing.*

Money Makers

He who gathers money little by little makes it grow.

PROVERBS 13:11

Are your children at the age where they would like to start earning money? It is such an important step as they mature and learn greater responsibility. And you will love the freedom of saying "maybe you can save up for _____ with your own money." I have some simple money-making ideas for your children. And trust me—these are Barnes family tested!

A toy sale is the children's version of a garage sale! Keep the prices low and then let the children take it from there. It will teach them about making change, negotiating, and, after sitting and waiting for customers, perseverance! They will become excited about gathering items to sell, and they will feel the independence of pocket money.

Dog walking in a safe environment is a great way for kids to earn some extra money. Our kids became birthday party helpers for $3.00 an hour. They passed out food, rounded up trash, and even helped with the games. I just heard of a junior high youth group that raised $24,000 for the children of Nepal by having "Bible reading marathons" with sponsors who donated money for their hours of reading. It's amazing what kids will do when they're motivated!

Simple Pleasures

- Avoid sentences such as "we cannot afford that." A child does not need that information.
- Show children how you base decisions on values, need, and being a good steward.
- Money is important, but don't let money talk take over your family time.

Wisdom for Living

I want to teach my children the value of hard work.
I want them to feel the satisfaction that comes with relying
on You, Lord, and seeing Your faithfulness every day.

Making Light

Your word is a lamp to my feet and a light for my path.

PSALM 119:105

God is a God of light. When we accept Christ, we have that light within us. Find ways to express that light outwardly. It is something to share, not to hide. Show it in action, word, deed, attitude, and perspective. And show it in your home by "making light" with candles, lamps, and other bright ideas. You might have dark spots in your home that could be more comforting with a little light.

Lighting is one of the most important ingredients in making any home beautiful and comfortable. Let your imagination take over with special lamps, mood-setting lighting with twinkles, firelight, and warm-colored bulbs. Use miniature lamps, groupings of candles, and wall-mounted sconces. I even have candles in my kitchen. Look around you for "shining examples" of lamps and shades.

Now, how can you share your light with another person today? Is there someone with the need of friendship, love, kindness, or cheer? You can light up your neighborhood by hosting simple teas or times to talk. Invite the neighborhood kids over to play for an afternoon and give their moms a breather. What a light you will be!

Light! It's wonderful. It so reminds me of the "light" we can be in the world—to our friends and our neighbors—as we "glow" with the love of Christ!

Simple Pleasures

- Light a candle while your children take a bath.
- Sip tea or cocoa in the early morning as the sun comes up. Catch the first light of the day.
- Replace your high-wattage bulbs with lower, more efficient ones.

Wisdom for Living

Let me be a light in my family, my neighborhood, and my world.
Let Your light surround me and remind me each day
to stand tall and share You, Lord.

A Good Record

From everyone who has been given much, much will be required.

LUKE 12:48

Throwing away records that later turn out to be important can cause a lot of work and worry. If this is not your "thing," I have a few guidelines for good record keeping. I've come up with a seven-step plan. Give it a try and see if it makes your life simpler.

1. Know what to keep for permanent records and "current circumstance" records.
2. Keep it simple.
3. Set aside a spot for your records. Use something fireproof.
4. Tell someone where your records are in case of an emergency.
5. Seek professional help for records dealing with tax purposes.
6. Change your record-keeping system when you make a life change.
7. Set aside time for your record keeping—once a month is ideal.

The goal of simple record keeping is to reduce stress in our lives and to give us more time for the really important things God has for us to do! If your system or lack of a system keeps you busy searching for papers or bills or important records, it is time to take time getting a better system in place. You will be thrilled with the results.

Simple Pleasures

- Copy a monthly schedule of activities so everyone knows what's going on.
- Keep receipts in one place in your wallet to make returns easy.
- Process incoming bills as they come in so you spend money on needs, not on late fees.

Wisdom for Living

Give me the frame of mind to simplify my life, Lord.
I don't want clutter to invade my home or my heart.
Help me manage well all that You have blessed me with.

October

KEEPING UP AND KEEPING THE FAITH

A Friend You Already Have

Think about a friend you already have. Can a sister be a friend? Or a mother or daughter? What about a colleague or a teacher? What about a husband? One of the most beautiful things about friendship is that it crosses categories and roles. In fact, you never know when a person wearing one name tag in your life—grandma, niece, neighbor, child's teacher, pastor's wife, casual acquaintance—might step over her label and sign up as a treasured friend of the heart.

There's a mystery to the ways of friendship. After all, finding a friend is like discovering a treasure. Maybe it is someone you encounter each day, the mom of your child's friend at school, the librarian, the letter carrier. Who knows! Finding a friend in someone you already love is like finding a treasure in the rafters of your own attic. It's one of life's most joyful surprises! Just when you are praying for a friend, chances are God has one already in your life's circle just waiting to be discovered.

Simple Pleasures

* Make a list of the good friends you have had in your life. Praise God for them.
* Pray for strengthened friendships and healing in relationships that need mending.
* Call your sister or brother and thank them for their friendship.

Wisdom for Living

God, I could use a good friend right now. Please show me someone who offers friendship, and let me offer my friendship in return.

Life Is Richer with Maturity

Solid food is for those who are mature, who have trained themselves to recognize the difference between right and wrong and then do what is right.

HEBREWS 5:14

God doesn't want us to remain spiritually immature! I want to share with you some thoughts about aging. Who wants to think about it, right? Well, it happens. And there are many blessings that go along with entering the stage of life I am in. One of those blessings is that I can pass along some wisdom I gained with hindsight to you!

Many of the 30- to 40-year-old women I meet seem to dwell on how old they are. I always assure them that each season of life has much to offer. Life becomes richer the more mature we become. You know yourself better. You understand how God has worked in your life, and you can share that with others. Simple times with family mean so much more.

In our Christian walk, we're encouraged to wean ourselves off of spiritual baby food and grow into solid foods (read Hebrews 5:11-14). God wants us to exhibit signs of maturity. And many times this comes through very difficult situations. If we're just "Sunday Christians," we'll never grow to maturity. It takes the study of the Bible to become "meat eaters" of God's Word. Here's a simple tip: Take a book of the Bible and begin reading a little each day. Give yourself the chance to grow!

Simple Pleasures

- Read a bit of Scripture right before bed. Even just two verses a night.
- Get your children into the Word by reading it before a family meal.
- Set out a children's Bible in your home so visiting children can read it.

Wisdom for Living

Lord, thank You for the life I have had so far. I am so excited about what is yet to come. I want my faith to grow deeper and my life richer. Praise You, Lord.

The Secret of Success

Have faith in the LORD your God and you will be upheld.

2 CHRONICLES 20:20

Do you need encouragement to finish a particular task or take action on something your heart has been nudging you to do? It is the action or project you think of every time you have a spare moment. Then the inspiration and the moment are gone and you think "someday I will have the time to do it and do it right."

What you need is the secret of success. If you're like me, you want to know how a project is going to turn out before you pour your heart and soul into it. Will it be a success? Will it be worth my while? But you know, success is not really our responsibility. We're just called to do what God asks: witness for Him, help those in need, and live lives of integrity. And we're to leave the outcome to Him! We may never know the results of our caring deeds. Or we may have the joy of seeing what our "seeds" have done. Either way, our job is to be faithful and obedient. Our God will do the rest. Pretty simple, wouldn't you say?

Today, try to make room for whatever God is calling, nudging, or directing you to do. You might be surprised by how successful you feel by the end of the day.

Simple Pleasures

- What is God calling you to do? Think with your heart today.
- Look up encouragement in a concordance and reflect on God's Word.
- Spend ten minutes sitting near a river or lake.

Wisdom for Living

O God, I want Your view of success in everything I do.
May I never hold back out of fear of failure. Please help me see
that You work miracles through the frailties of Your children.

Pass It On

> *We ought always to thank God for you, brothers, and rightly so, because your faith is growing more and more, and the love every one of you has for each other is increasing.*

> 2 THESSALONIANS 1:3

Aren't the simple teaching of values and the sharing of our faith in God, two of the prime reasons for establishing a home? In everything you do, let the way you live be an example of a holy life that is pleasing to the Lord.

When I'm serving a tea party to my grandchildren, I'm passing on the value of manners, the beauty of small rituals, and the joy of spending time together. When Bob reads Bible stories to our grandchildren or works with them in the garden, he's passing along a deep faith, a love of growing things, and a respect for hard work. We're teaching them what it means to be healthy adult men and women. These are lessons only taught through the way we live. It's the essence of why I think a child-friendly home is vital not just to our happiness but to the spiritual future of our children. It's such a simple concept—but so important!

Let your actions be an example of God in your life. When it comes to influencing children, your actions do speak as loudly as words. What are you telling your children or grandchildren about a good life, an abundant life, in the activities you share with them?

Simple Pleasures

- Have a ritual of lighting a candle when you decide to "pass on" a privilege to a child.
- Consider what you are passing on to your children that you do not want to.
- Ponder the sweetness of treasured memories in your heart.

Wisdom for Living

Dear Father, how I want to pass along a tradition of faith and values. Let me always be aware of what I am "telling" a child through my every action. Lord, help me tell them about You.

The Model Woman

I tell you the truth, anyone who has faith in me will do what I have been doing. He will do even greater things than these, because I am going to the Father.

JOHN 14:12

Along our walk with the Lord, where do we go these days to find a model for the kind of woman God has in mind? I look at television, and I can't find her there. I look in magazines. Not there either! But I see her depicted beautifully in the pages of Scripture. Proverbs 31 is a picture of a woman I can be proud of. "Strength and honor are her clothing" (verse 25 NKJV). "She opens her mouth in wisdom, and on her tongue is the law of kindness" (verse 16 NKJV). With the help of our Lord, we can be that kind of woman.

Study this section of Scripture with a heart open to change. For seeds of real transformation to grow, you first might have to give up a false image of what you should be. Or even what you want to be. I don't mean give up on your dreams, but be sure you are not trying to live up to an image of a mother, wife, or woman that is not the one God designed.

Are you ready to discover who God created you to be? Embrace His Word and let it give you new vision for the many strengths and blessings of real, godly womanhood. Your new model is a beautiful one. A holy one. And one created in the image of God.

Simple Pleasures

- Compliment yourself on one of your strengths.
- Thank God for creating you as a unique individual.
- Pray for guidance to become the woman He created you to be.

Wisdom for Living

Please, Lord, guard my mouth from the evils of gossip and hatred. Show me how to be disciplined and how to live with integrity. Help me be the kind of woman I can look up to, the kind who pleases You!

Right in Front of Your Nose

"You will seek me and find me when you seek me with all your heart. I will be found by you," declares the LORD.

JEREMIAH 29:13-14

People today might make the search for God complex, but really it is quite simple. Even believers can make seeking God much more difficult than it really is. You know, He's really not that hard to find!

I don't know about your husband, but my Bob can't find anything in the kitchen without calling out, "Emilie where's the...!" I go to the cupboard and it's right there. It might be hiding a bit behind the sugar canister or it might be in plain view—he just didn't see it. I think we sometimes miss seeing God in this same way. He isn't stuck in some corner or behind layers of confusing philosophy or theology. He's out in the bright light of day—and even in the darkness of night. And yet we occasionally have a hard time seeing what's right in front of our nose.

Don't give up searching. It isn't a game of hide-and-seek; God's objective is not to elude you. He is everywhere. The problem is with your seeing, not with His presence. He's been there all the time, and He cannot wait for your eyes to be opened to His love.

Simple Pleasures

* Reach out and touch God. He is right beside you and within your heart.
* Ask God to reveal Himself to you if you are facing a time of darkness or distance.
* Ask someone to pray for you. Be vulnerable before the Lord.

Wisdom for Living

Help me to see You, Lord. Your presence is evident in all of creation and in every aspect of my life. I am forgiven and I am saved because You are real.

Order Is a Spiritual Thing

> Everything should be done in a fitting and orderly way.
>
> 1 CORINTHIANS 14:40

God delights in turning weaknesses into strengths and bringing order out of confusion! Goodness knows that in our day-to-day life we offer Him great delight, don't we? But a home filled with the laughter of children is also filled with chaos.

When we're "in order," we have smoother communication, more effective problem solving, better task management, better relationships, and a better idea of what needs to be done. I receive hundreds of letters from women wanting to get organized. It starts with you! Getting organized is an investment of time initially, but it is worth it. And the process also teaches you about your own priorities, your needs, and God's design for your life.

Make sure everything has a designated space. Get rid of what you don't use. Remember, the end result is to give you more available time—time to do God's will for your life. I love this little saying: "People before things, people before projects, family before friends, husband before children, husband before parents, tithe before wants, Bible before opinions, Jesus before all."

Simple Pleasures

* For fast recycling, have separate containers for plastics, newspapers, and soda cans.
* Create a brightly colored file for your important documents. It will be easy to locate.
* Have a drawer for batteries, candles, and matches for access during power outages.

Wisdom for Living

Jesus, I put You before all! Let my confusion become order, and may it show the world Your sovereignty.

The Wonder of God

Be strong and courageous. Do not be afraid or terrified because of them, for the LORD your God goes with you; he will never leave you nor forsake you.

DEUTERONOMY 31:6

As a little girl who was afraid to talk in front of others, I had no idea that God would use me to touch the lives of thousands through speaking! I want to encourage you by sharing about the wonder of God in my life. It relates to your life, because God can and is transforming your fears and weaknesses into testimonies of His grace, mercy, and love.

When God began to use me through speaking and writing, I was shocked. It only happened when God saw a willingness in my spirit to be used by Him. Am I still nervous when I get up to speak? Yes. I still have to rely on Him each time I open my mouth. I often wonder as I look out on the faces of an audience, "Why me, Lord? There are many better speakers and writers than I am." But you know what? God always answers back with the words He spoke to Moses, "Now therefore, go, and I will be with your mouth and teach you what to say" (Exodus 4:12).

Are you already thinking of a similar area of your life? Do you feel God tugging at your heart to follow a certain pursuit but have been unwilling to risk the failure? It is hard to take risks. But it is not really a risk when it is God's calling in your life. Listen for it and be open to its transforming power when the time comes.

Simple Pleasures

* Just before you go to sleep, think about how God is mighty and powerful in your life.
* Do something today that scares you a little. Stretch yourself.
* Let God be God in all your circumstances.

Wisdom for Living

*Show me the way to be a vessel for You, Lord. I am scared.
You know my heart, so I will trust You with my life.
I am ready to witness Your strength and Your power in my life.*

Precious Moments

We proclaim to you what we have seen and heard, so that you may have fellowship with us. And our fellowship is with the Father and with his Son, Jesus Christ. We write this to make our joy complete.

1 JOHN 1:3-4

In your daily life, I encourage you to stick close to God's people. Some of my most precious moments of Christian friendship have happened within my own family—times of sharing with Bob over breakfast and sweet times of prayer tucking a child into bed. And what blessings have come when five or six of us have gathered for a home Bible study or a time of prayer! It's during these occasions when we really get down to business in our lives. So many times I've prayed and wept—and laughed and hugged—over a cup of afternoon tea with a friend. What a privilege to pray together. What a joy to support one another in seasons of crisis and need. Such amazing things happen when we choose to reach out to one another in sustaining love!

When do you feel the strength of Christian friendship? Find ways to re-create that fellowship even beyond your church family. Make it a part of daily living and with friends, family members, and maybe even with a group of other mothers in your neighborhood who would like the encouragement of fellowship.

It's such a simple concept, isn't it? Sharing your thoughts about the fellowship that takes place in your home is a way to get your family excited about Christian living. And your children will understand early on how important fellowship is.

Simple Pleasures

- Be a spiritual support for a friend through prayer, encouragement, and care.
- Express kindness to a stranger today.
- Have your children pray for other children.

Wisdom for Living

What a gift it is to spend time with believers, Lord. I thank You for those you have brought into my life. May I seek fellowship with my own family and nurture that fellowship daily.

Responding to Order

> *He will wipe every tear from their eyes. There will be no more death or mourning or crying or pain, for the old order of things has passed away.*
>
> REVELATION 21:4

I don't know about you, but I respond positively to order in my life. I believe it's because we're made in the image of God. He's the ultimate organizer! And the results of His ordering Spirit are always good. Begin with your heart. As we open ourselves to God, putting Him first in our lives, He will show us little ways to organize the chaos surrounding us and leading us into a more peaceful, ordered existence.

It takes time. Growing in the Spirit is a lifelong process! Pray with me, "Lord, I seek Your order in my life. Place Your priorities on my heart as I invest my time and energy today. May these efforts all reflect Your perfect will and way. You are first in my life, Lord. I pray I remember this each new day and that I will be pleasing to You as I see order in my life." Spend time in His Word today. Read some of Genesis and Revelation and think about God's all-powerful order and His loving intentions for us.

Simple Pleasures

- Get rid of some piles of "stuff" today.
- Throw away ten pieces of paper.
- Pray for your priorities to become clear. Pray for this daily.

Wisdom for Living

I seek You today, Lord. I want to sense the security of having my life and my home in order. Let my children feel Your presence in the calm of their surroundings.

What a Bright Idea

Put your trust in the light while you have it, so that you may become sons of light.

JOHN 12:36

Lights! Action! Decoration! Lighting is one of the easiest ways to decorate beautifully on a budget. It may be natural light from windows or skylights or lamps, chandeliers, even candles.

Right now, where you are sitting, what light source is affecting the area? Could you use another lamp? There are so many fun ways to create your own lamps. A friend of mine used a large bowling trophy. Well, I might have to think about that one! What do you have that could be transformed into a useful ray of light to read by, talk by, or pray by? How bright or soft do you want certain corners or areas of a room? Think about how you might use an area differently if you changed the light source for a corner.

Another source of lovely, soft light in areas of your home is a set of tiny white twinkle lights. These are wonderful all year long, so this next Christmas, just leave them up. Small as they are, they give off an amazing amount of light. It makes me think of how God uses each one of us!

Simple Pleasures

- Buy some decorative soaps for your guest bathroom.
- Place fragrant potpourri in stuffy closets to add freshness.
- Use low-wattage lightbulbs wherever your family spends time relaxing.

Wisdom for Living

You are the Light of the world, Lord. May I seek to see my life as it is cast in the brilliance of Your light.

Home Robbers

I will say of the LORD, "He is my refuge and my fortress, my God, in whom I trust."

PSALM 91:2

Do you long for a home that's warm and welcoming, comfortable and freeing? If you're anything like me, you want a home that reflects your personality and renews your soul, a home that reflects who you are spiritually, a home that glows with the spirit of loveliness. No matter how little or how much you have, you can experience the results of a godly home. You can stop the home robbers at the curb! Make your prayer today, "Father God, there are so many people who want to steal the joy of my home. I want to cherish my family and friends, those who build up my desire to reflect Your spirit of loveliness in my home." Amen!

When a child is negative or disrespectful, pray for their attitude and for their heart to change. Be a prayer warrior for every member of your family and for your home. Ask God to guide your decisions in all matters, from finances to disciplining your child. Seek His wisdom so that you can protect your home with the balance God calls you to have in your life and family.

Use your home for wonderful, nurturing gatherings that celebrate all who enter it. Welcome guests into your embrace and build them up. This love and kindness is a cornerstone for every solid home.

Simple Pleasures

- Arm yourself with the Word of God and protect your home from spiritual laziness.
- Focus on the needs of your child that might be hiding behind a rebellious façade.
- Talk about your children with your spouse. Plan a day to go for a walk and share.

Wisdom for Living

Lord, I pray for Your protection. May You help us guard our hearts and our home to preserve the joy and innocence of Your children.

Shield and Defender

> Be on your guard; stand firm in the faith; be men of courage; be strong.
>
> 1 CORINTHIANS 16:13

When we pray in faith to the Lord, we realize He keeps His children safe and secure. Even when the situation—whether that be personal or one affecting our nation—seems overwhelming, we know our hiding place is in the Lord. A shield was very valuable in time of battle, and we are certainly in a battle. But because we believe and trust in God's character, we can have a song of joy.

God is a holy being. It sets Him aside from all other creatures. Psalm 33:20-21 says: "We depend upon the Lord alone to save us. Only he can help us; he protects us like a shield. No wonder we are happy in the Lord! For we are trusting in him. We trust his holy name" (TLB). We cannot find this power in human measures of protection or strength.

Are you looking to God to ease your worries and anxieties? Or are you looking for reassurance in earthly things? The peace that comes with complete trust in the Lord is like nothing you have ever encountered. Maybe your worry is not of national security. Maybe it is about sickness, despair, or finances. These all belong in the hands of the Lord. He waits with open arms. His palms are open to accept what it is that weighs on your heart. Give it over to Him. Trust Him.

Simple Pleasures

- Keep a prayer journal, and see exactly how God works in your life!
- In the midst of trials, spend additional time reading your Bible to boost your faith.
- Recite comforting Scripture verses, like Jeremiah 29:11, to help your heart embrace God's faithfulness.

Wisdom for Living

Lord, I trust You with everything that is worrying me today. Nothing is too small or too huge for You to handle. You are my Savior.

Hanging Around

I run in the paths of your commands, for you have set my heart free.

PSALM 119:32

Tradition says that wall decorations should be hung at about eye level. I'm here to set you free! Try hanging a picture higher or lower than expected. High over a bookcase, for example. Place a little shelf and a small picture close to a plant. Think of the charm of a Raggedy Ann doll in a child's rocking chair enjoying her own eye-level miniature painting. Take a piece of art and set it on a shelf or table and just let it lean against the wall. Find matting that is in contrast to your wall color. Grab a fun frame, pull out the backing, insert a beautiful piece of tissue paper, and hang it so it reaches high up on a window. This stained glass look is lovely.

The bottom line is: be creative. Shake it up. Let yourself have fun with creating a home you love to live in. You don't have to follow trends or rules. Go with what looks and feels right for the particular room.

Break out of the box, and you'll be amazed at what you discover. That's true with life as well as with decorating!

Simple Pleasures

* Do something really drastic. Turn your worry over to God.
* Read a hymn today, and let your mind linger on its message.
* Raise your voice in praise of God.

Wisdom for Living

Shake up my perspective today, Lord. How can I see the world as filled with limitless possibilities? Please show me.

A Decorating Story

Greet those who love us in the faith. Grace be with you all.

TITUS 3:15

I spent the first half of my grown-up life as a homemaker and mother and the second half running a business with my husband. Yet the home Bob and I decorated together has been featured in *Better Homes and Gardens.* Who, us? How did we get to that point? I began as most do—with nothing and going from there! I have to add that the beauty and interest of our decorating is as much to Bob's credit as to mine. The whole idea has been to make it a beautiful place of love and comfort, a place to entertain new and old friends. And definitely a place that says "God is part of who we are and how we live!"

Now, I certainly didn't expect my home to appear on the cover of a magazine, but I have always expected that my home would be seen by the One who matters. Always I asked myself if He would be comfortable with the feel of my home. Would He be pleased by how I used our house for His glory? And whether Bob and I had very little or enough to pay for new wallpaper or carpet, the answer was always yes. God would be pleased. This is a home of love and caring. It is a home that is founded on the love of the Lord.

Simple Pleasures

- Think big by praying about the small things.
- Is there an opportunity in the works for you? Pay close attention.
- List your goals as a wife, mother, and woman of God.

Wisdom for Living

*Teach me Your ways, Lord, that I might always have
a home that pleases You, lifts You up, and shares You
with the people who enter my door.*

Imagination

We live by faith, not by sight.

2 CORINTHIANS 5:7

I love decorating children's rooms. Enjoy this chance to play with ideas while your children are still at home. Don't miss out on what can become a great memory for you and your child as you work together and have some simple fun.

You can let your imagination go to so many wonderful places. Try to provide a living space that encourages children to draw, paint, build, act, and create. Give them an easel with a bucketful of crayons or chalk. Bless them with a lap desk or a small table and chairs. Paint one wall with high-gloss enamel so they can draw on the walls. Place beanbag chairs, comfortable cushions, cozy fleece blankets wherever there is room. Hook up one of those retractable clothing lines so that you can stretch it out and drape a blanket over it as an instant tent. Keep the line retracted when not in use so that it isn't a hazard. Add a basket of books and toys that is low to the ground so that the children can help with cleanup.

What are your child's favorite activities? Work those themes into the room so you can celebrate his interests. Decorating your child's room is truly a wonderful opportunity to shape his environment. And shape his life. What a great place to spend time reading Bible stories and answering his incredible questions.

Learn to feel your creativity and don't just rely on your sight. It is a lot like your faith in God! Trust His leading in your life.

Simple Pleasures

- Spend time with your child in his room today. Listen to music and enjoy the space.
- Over coffee, draw up some plans for redecorating a room in the future.
- Recall one thing you enjoyed most about a childhood room.

Wisdom for Living

Father, I will embrace the fun of creating with childlike wonder.
I will see You in the smile on my child's face.

Being an Example

In everything set them an example by doing what is good.

TITUS 2:7

Are we consistent with what we say we believe? That is a tough one no matter who you are. But it is especially important when you are a mom. Have you ever had your unkind words or expressions come back to you in a miniature reenactment through your child? Oh, what a sinking feeling. But of course, being consistent in behavior, attitude, and discipline is not just important because you have children. It is important because you are a child of God.

Our children and others are watching to see how we behave when no one is looking. If we talk calmness and patience, how do we respond when standing in a slow line at the market? How does our conversation go when there's a slowdown on the highway? Do we help people out even when it's not convenient? We are continually setting some kind of example whether we know it or not. Be a good neighbor today. Send out a thank-you card to someone who's done something for you. Call a friend or send an e-mail. Let your life be a simple example to all those around you.

And when your children get older and you are standing in the store alone, growing impatient in the ten-item line, remember that God is always watching. Do not disappoint Him. Make Him proud of His child today.

Simple Pleasures

- Listen to your words. Watch your actions. Your children do!
- Apologize to your child if you need to.
- Model love and acceptance by treating people fairly.

Wisdom for Living

Lord, I need Your guidance to be a role model for my children.
Help me to always be an example of a Christian, a godly woman.
Let them never doubt my integrity.

Shine Like a Star

Those who are wise will shine like the brightness of the heavens, and those who lead many to righteousness, like the stars for ever and ever.

DANIEL 12:3

I want you to be a star! Quite simply, be a light that leads people to Jesus. That might sound a little intimidating, but think about it with me. Does your life light up your home? Do your children and grandchildren reflect the love and warmth you've given them? Do people say you make a difference in their lives? We all have "star potential"! We each have 24 hours a day and seven days to the week. Think about what you will do with your time.

Explore the ideas in your mind and the tuggings on your heart. All of the great conquests of life have started as a little idea in someone's head. You don't want to ignore the path God has set before you. What are your deepest dreams? Writing a song, starting a business, authoring a book, helping children? Reach out and plan how you're going to energize that thought into reality. Encourage this same exploration in the lives of your children. They will appreciate this later as they strive to define themselves and their heart's desires. Get them to dream big and set goals.

As Christians we either grow, rising heavenward, or we fall toward earth. Reach for your home in the sky. Be a star.

Simple Pleasures

- Create a wish list of ways you hope to shine in your lifetime.
- Set three small goals for the next three months. Work toward them with a full heart.
- Ask God for direction in your pursuits. What wonderful ideas does He have in mind?

Wisdom for Living

Lord, You place on my heart the dreams and interests that make me special in Your sight. Help me to understand these and fill my life with Your hope for this child of Yours.

The God of All Grace

Therefore, the promise comes by faith, so that it may be by grace and may be guaranteed to all Abraham's offspring—not only to those who are of the law but also to those who are of the faith of Abraham.

ROMANS 4:16

Count on it. From time to time your teacup is going to overflow! Pull up a comfortable chair and let's talk about God's grace. Could there be anything more wonderful to discuss with a friend?

The apostle Peter tells us that "the God of all grace...will himself restore you and make you strong, firm and steadfast" (1 Peter 5:10). There are going to be some dark shadows. But even at those times, your cup will overflow with God's goodness and mercy. How do I know? I've been there. I've experienced God's grace in the midst of the worst four years of my life as I battled cancer. And now, when the clouds are lifting, I see so much more clearly. I see how I've been restored and strengthened. It didn't happen exactly the way I thought it would. But you know, the results were so much deeper—and much more wonderful—than I could imagine.

Look for God's grace in your life. Turn your eyes toward it and widen your arms to embrace it. Grace is what gives us wholeness, hope, and strength. As deep as the pain might be that you or someone you love is experiencing, God's grace is so much greater, deeper, and lasting. See how great it is to talk about grace?

Simple Pleasures

- Extend grace to a friend who needs to experience it.
- Explain grace to your children so they understand their heavenly Father's love.
- Spend some quiet time in a comfortable chair. Think of God embracing you.

Wisdom for Living

God, I feel Your grace in my life. It touches all that I do.
It fills my heart with the joy of receiving a great gift. You are my Lord.

Table Talk

Now go; I will help you speak and will teach you what to say.

EXODUS 4:12

Solomon said, "Better a dry crust with peace and quiet than a house full of feasting, with strife" (Proverbs 17:11). Solomon was sooo right! But how does a busy mom go about creating a more relaxed mealtime? Careful planning sure helps. Let's explore some easy ways to enhance your home dining experience.

Keep the food simple and matched to the needs of your family. Serving difficult-to-handle food to small children invites disaster. Conversation can be lively, but put off weighty matters or emotional issues for another time. And mealtime is not the time to bring up discipline issues. Put on some good music as a background.

The most meaningful and effective way to bring peace to the dinner table is to invite God to be present. Make it a habit at your house. Hold hands and ask the Lord's blessing on the meal and on those gathered around your table. Have your children take turns offering the blessing. Continue the spirit of thanksgiving as you partake in the meal. Explore with your children the ways God has blessed each of you that day. Or list all of the people you would invite to a special meal if you could. Don't just share a meal with your family, share your life. And give it to God.

Simple Pleasures

- Write short meal prayers on index cards and include them in your child's school lunch.
- Post Scripture on your refrigerator so you think on God's Word as you prepare meals.
- Grow a few vegetables in your yard this year. Enjoy the bounty!

Wisdom for Living

Lord, I invite you to be at our table for each meal.
Help us to recognize the importance of eating together as a family.
May our words be pleasing to You.

Believe What God Believes

May the God of hope fill you with
all joy and peace as you trust in
him, so that you may overflow
with hope by the power of the
Holy Spirit.

ROMANS 15:13

When life becomes difficult or even when daily stresses get to you, it could be that you are living by your own theology. The gospel according to you. And believe me, that is not a good direction. Truth is, you are probably much harder on yourself, or more negative about things, than God would ever be. Believe what God believes about *you!* Here are some simple thoughts to take with you today:

- Because God loves you, He is slow to lose patience with you.

- Because God loves you, He doesn't treat you as an object to be manipulated.

- Because God loves you, He is for you.

- Because God loves you, He keeps working patiently with you—even when you feel like giving up.

- Because God loves you, He never says there's no hope for you. No, He patiently works with you, loves you, and disciplines you.

Simple Pleasures

For God so loved the world that he gave his one and only Son,
that whoever believes in him shall not perish but have eternal life.
For God did not send his Son into the world to condemn the world,
but to save the world through him.

—JOHN 3:16-17

Wisdom for Living

God, I want to wake up each morning and embrace
the thought that You love me. I want to believe it wholly.
I want to believe what You believe about my life.

November

GRACIOUS COMFORT

A Work in Progress

Praise be to the God and Father of our Lord Jesus Christ, the Father of compassion and the God of all comfort.

2 CORINTHIANS 1:3

A few simple thoughts on appreciation! Growing in godliness is a life-long process. I want to continue to seek God on a daily basis so He can direct my feet along His path. Psalm 100:3 says: "Know that the LORD is God. It is he who made us, and we are his; we are his people, the sheep of his pasture." That is such a comforting fact to rest in. We are God's people. Do you forget that when worries about your "to do" list or your mortgage consume you? Do you forget to take comfort in being a child of God?

Know this and appreciate it. Let yourself live your life following the One who leads you safely home. Let me leave you today with this prayer of simple appreciation: "Father God, thank You for reminding me that it's the little things that count in life. Let me dwell on this truth today. I sometimes get so caught up in the big things, the big worries, the big picture that I forget the preciousness of simplicity. Amen." God has made it clear that He is interested in His children. What an awesome God we have!

Simple Pleasures

* Tell God what you most appreciate about Him.
* List what you think God most appreciates about you this week.
* Take time with your children to explain how you are all children of God.

Wisdom for Living

Mighty God, You lead us. You guide us.
You are the Giver of life. Thank You.

Anchoring a Room

I have sought your face with all my heart; be gracious to me according to your promise.

PSALM 119:58

When you return home from an afternoon out, does crossing your threshold bring you refreshment? Does it send a message of comfort at first glance? Make your home a little more beautiful and peaceful with a few simple decorating tips.

Where does your eye fall first when you enter a room? Whatever that item is, that's your focal point. It's the room's anchor, the item that sets the tone or the mood for the whole room. If that item is a pile of laundry or toys, it might be time for a change.

Do you have an art print, a family heirloom, or a collection you absolutely love? That can be your focal point. Give your special item a place of honor and arrange the rest of the room to call attention to it. Play around with the arrangement of your furniture to give it all a new eye. Transformation of your living space doesn't require the purchase of a new rug or end table. All it takes is a bit of rearranging and a shift of visual perspective.

You'll be surprised how lovely and comforting the "new" room will feel.

Simple Pleasures

- Start a gratitude journal.
- Have lots of cozy blankets resting on chairs and draped over beds.
- Set up candles everywhere. Their visual warmth brings comfort on cold evenings.

Wisdom for Living

*Lord, I seek Your creativity in all that I do. I search nature
for the colors made by You because I long to bring
that beauty into the home You have given me.*

A Place You Love to Be

You will receive a rich welcome into the eternal kingdom of our Lord and Savior Jesus Christ.

2 PETER 1:11

Your kitchen is the heart of your home. Make it a place you love to be. Make it the place your children and their friends feel welcome and loved. The key to making the best of any kitchen—spacious or tiny—is to make efficient use of the space you have.

By the time they are 45, most women will have spent more than 50,000 hours in the kitchen. Amazing, isn't it? If you are already there, you know how important the feel of a kitchen is to your well-being. And if you still have quite a few hours to clock in before you reach that total, you will appreciate these simple ideas for years to come. It doesn't take a major remodeling to make your kitchen a room you can thoroughly enjoy. A fresh paint job, some plants or flowers, new knobs on the cabinet doors, or just a thorough cleaning and rearranging. New shelf paper in a pretty design will make you smile every time you open a cupboard. Fill a bowl with bright lemons, limes, or any fruit in season and create a useful still life piece of art for your counter.

What about a radio on a shelf or even a tiny TV? And a simple rule of thumb? Make it a place that says "Come on in. You are always welcome."

Simple Pleasures

- Place something special in the kitchen that is for your pleasure. A vase, candle, or lamp.
- Clean the countertops of clutter and enjoy the white space.
- Have on hand air freshener in a pleasant scent for the holidays.

Wisdom for Living

Father, let Your light shine in the heart of my home.
I desire to fill the space around me with symbols of Your joy.

Child Friendly

I praise you, Father, Lord of heaven and earth, because you have hidden these things from the wise and learned, and revealed them to little children.

MATTHEW 11:25

Make your home a place where children love to be! Do your children feel at home in your house? Do visiting children sense they are welcomed guests? Let me share a few easy ideas to make your home child friendly.

Children love to play with "real stuff." Offer them some tools of their own and then supervise as necessary. Also, children appreciate beauty, and they love being treated like grown-ups. If a child comes to stay, put a vase of fresh flowers in their room just the way you would with adults. Read to your children. There are so many wonderful books out there for kids of all ages. Better yet, buy a blank book and encourage your child to write their own children's book with your help. They will really love the chance to illustrate the story!

For visiting children, have a child-friendly puzzle already in progress and out in the open so even a shy child will be encouraged to work on it. Children who visit us love to take their own decorated sack lunches outside while the adults enjoy lunch. Someone has said: "Simply as a little child, we learn a home is made from love." Let God's love be poured out on a child through you today.

Simple Pleasures

- Spend time recalling your favorite childhood memories.
- Draw a picture of your childhood home.
- When the children are gone, sit down and color in a coloring book. It's relaxing!

Wisdom for Living

Children should feel safe and loved. Lord, bless this home. Make it a haven for children. Let this be a place where children witness Your love for them.

Meant to Be Shared

Since you are eager to have spiritual gifts, try to excel in gifts that build up the church.

1 CORINTHIANS 14:12

Take some time today to reflect on two important questions: "What are my gifts?" and "What does it mean to serve others?" God intends for us to fill the cups of others the best way we know how and the best way we can. So often our "best way" is through our gifts, talents, and abilities. Recognizing these unique gifts is not a prideful activity. It is really a way to connect with how God is calling us to serve others. And when we do, the sweetness of His love and peace flows from cup to cup to cup.

I would never have guessed when I was a young wife many years ago that I would write books and conduct large seminars telling women how to get organized, how to care for a home, how to love their families, and how to live as a woman of God. I didn't feel adequate to tell anyone what to do! But over the years, as I've used my gifts I've felt God's grace overflow in my own life as well. The Bible tells us to use whatever gift we have received to serve others! Bless you today.

Simple Pleasures

- Discuss spiritual gifts with a mentor or friend.
- Thank the Lord today for the gifts He has blessed your children with.
- If you have a gift you haven't used in a while, dust it off and get creative with it.

Wisdom for Living

Help me to see the gifts You have planted in my heart, Lord. And today and every day to follow, let me use these gifts to serve others in Your name.

The Gift of a Memory

I will perpetuate your memory through all generations; therefore the nations will praise you for ever and ever.

PSALM 45:17

You know how precious time is. And so do others. That is why the very best gifts are gifts of your time that come with a memory attached. Give it as a treasure to the people you love! Explore ways to use your time to brighten someone's day.

Write a letter on a special occasion and save it to give to the recipient later. One mother I know wrote a letter to her newborn, and she plans to mail it on her daughter's eighteenth birthday. You can write a love letter to your spouse. Place it somewhere and let him happen upon it by surprise. Jot down sweet comments your children make. This will be a source of joy for you in years to come.

Have family photographs copied and give them as gifts. Frame the photos or put them in albums. Take children on a "memory journey." Read them your favorite verses in Scripture. Help them find a verse to memorize. Nurture a family tradition like a reunion breakfast once a year or dinner at Thanksgiving or Christmastime. Plan a special ceremony to pass along an heirloom to a child or a friend. Take every opportunity to pass along the gift of your family heritage in a way that is memorable.

Simple Pleasures

- Journal about the spiritual heritage you have been given.
- Pray to your heavenly Father about the needs on your heart.
- Bake an apple pie and serve it up with vanilla ice cream and honey.

Wisdom for Living

Time passes so quickly, Lord. Help me make each moment and memory-in-the-making count. May each minute I live be a testimony to my heritage of deep faith in You.

Sure, I'll Pray for You

I call on you, O God, for you will answer me; give ear to me and hear my prayer.

PSALM 17:6

When someone asks you to pray for them, what do you say? If you're like me, you promise to pray and you have every intention of doing so. But do you ever forget? I sometimes do. That's why I'm grateful the "keep it simple" motto even applies to our prayer lives.

Get yourself a little notebook. Add a "Prayer Request" tab and start writing down those requests. I've seen people who've done this become excited as they saw how God worked in dealing with their prayer requests. All our prayers aren't answered with a yes. People die, couples get divorced, and cancer isn't always cured. But you begin to realize God is sovereign and He has a master plan for all our lives.

It is amazing how this practice opens the floodgates of prayer needs in your own life. As you begin to prayerfully consider your personal concerns, those of family and friends, and those of the nation and world, soon your first response to any situation is "I need to pray about this." A heart that turns easily to prayer is one blessed with intimacy with God.

Try keeping track of all those prayer needs by jotting them down. Join in the blessing of a disciplined prayer life!

Simple Pleasures

- Begin the day by praying with your spouse.
- Pray with expectation. Do not doubt.
- Offer encouragement for a friend by praying for their strength and courage.

Wisdom for Living

Lord, may I always be a woman of my word and a keeper of promises. I thank You for Your promises to love me unconditionally and to always listen to my prayers.

If Mama Ain't Happy...

May the righteous be glad and rejoice before God; may they be happy and joyful.

PSALM 68:3

There's an old Southern saying, "If Mama ain't happy—ain't nobody happy!"

The woman of the house almost always sets the tone for everyone else in the family. If she has a joyous, cheerful spirit, it spreads and practically lights up the home—especially during the holidays.

How do you go about cultivating a happy spirit? Not by being fake, that's for sure. You do it by setting aside time to focus on God's love. If you're going through a tough time, talk it out with friends or seek wise counseling. Pour out your soul in a journal and in prayer. Take time to nurture your heart and your body. Go on short or long walks while you sort through your mental list of scheduled activities, things to do, or even burdens on your heart. Use that time to talk to God. He is right there beside you already. He is listening. In fact, He is the best walking companion a mom could have.

Do these things so that when your husband and children come home you can put a smile on your face that is genuine. You'll feel better and so will everyone else. Happiness is contagious.

Simple Pleasures

The highest and most desirable state of the soul
is to praise God in celebration for being alive.

—LUCI SWINDOLL

Wisdom for Living

There are days when I don't feel happiness, Lord.
When this happens, I long to uncover Your joy in my life.
When I seek this, I always find it. You are my source of great happiness.

If Teacups Could Talk

I hope to visit you and talk with you face to face, so that our joy may be complete.

2 JOHN 12

Now, your idea of a relaxing moment is probably not to sit in on a history lesson, but I want to tell you the story behind the invention of the tea bag. It is fascinating, and it illustrates how a simple idea can change the world. (Or at least how the world makes tea.)

It began with an American tea merchant named Thomas Sullivan. He hit on the idea of giving samples to his customers in small silk pouches. Soon they discovered the pouches could be put directly in teapots. Orders began "pouring" in for tea packaged in "those little bags." Before long, tea bags had become widely accepted. And it was the Duchess of Bedford who first thought of tea and cakes to carry her through until dinnertime. We can thank her for the joys of tasting cookies, scones, and other sweets with a hot cup of tea.

A lot of time has passed since then, but some things do grow better with age. For me, tea is all tied up with times alone with God, with friends, and with family. Believe me, if my teacups could talk—after all these years—what wonderful things they could tell you about some very special moments.

If your teacups could talk, what would they say? I'll bet they would remind you to make sweet memories of teatime with friends a part of your personal history.

Simple Pleasures

- Research tea shops in your area.
- Choose one a month to visit with a friend.
- Fix up a small tray with tea necessities and you have an instant tea cart.

Wisdom for Living

You made the time, Lord. Now I will make the tea.
Let's spend the afternoon together. I will listen
as Your Word speaks to my heart.

The Wonder of a Tea Party

If we walk in the light, as he is in the light, we have fellowship with one another.

1 John 1:7

There's nothing quite like an old-fashioned tea party to bring friends together.

A friend told me recently to save an upcoming Saturday for a special gathering. She's planning a tea to celebrate her spiritual birthday and wants friends to join her.

Having tea together nurtures friendship by inviting us to be present—right now, in the moment. So much in our culture can be done without really being there, without being mentally and emotionally tuned to the people around us. Without moments of connection, it is easy to feel distant from anyone not directly involved in your day. Friends help us feel grounded and secure and connected to the body of Christ.

There's something about an old-fashioned tea party that gently invites us to feel safe. Tea parties are naturally comforting. They provide moments in which we can experience fellowship and the warmth of community. Believe me, it's not the tea! It's the spirit of the tea party. Take the time to enjoy being with kindred spirits over a cup of tea. It's both simple and wonderful.

Simple Pleasures

- Tell someone how thankful you are that they are in your life.
- Let the Lord know what you treasure most in your life.
- Listen to classical music today while you take care of business.

Wisdom for Living

I think of my own spiritual birthday and am filled with gratitude and joy. Your love, Lord, connects me to others. We celebrate being united as the body of Christ.

Are You Listening?

Comfort, comfort my people, says your God.

ISAIAH 40:1

Most of us have no difficulty talking. Listening is the hard part! I'm more than willing to give an opinion or offer advice—sometimes when it hasn't been requested! Have you ever spent the time someone is sharing from their heart to figure out what your response is going to be? Sometimes our communication problems aren't from talking but from talking too much!

In the Bible, James tells us that the tongue can be used for good or for bad—it's like a rudder steering us into stormy or peaceful situations (see James 3). I like to think of our words as silver boxes tied with bows. I like that because I can visualize husbands and wives giving lovely gifts of silver boxes to each other in their conversations. We're not to speak ugly words that tear down but words that are uplifting and encouraging—words that impart blessing.

Give yourself over to the act of listening next time someone is sharing with you. Maybe it will be your husband discussing work, or your son chatting away about why the blue marble is better than the green one. Maybe it will be God, expressing His love for you.

Simple Pleasures

* Listen more. Speak less.
* When you pray, focus not on what you are saying, but what is spoken in the silence.
* Play games with your children that develop their listening skills.

Wisdom for Living

Lord, I want to listen to those who need me. May I focus on their every word. Let my response be heard in my silent attention, without judgment and without personal objectives.

Cookies and Milk

You are my hiding place from every storm of life; you even keep me from getting into trouble.

PSALM 32:7 TLB

Whatever happened to homemade cookies and milk? They are the ultimate comfort food, in my opinion. And those moments enjoying such sweetness will become memories for a child. What comforts are you creating for you and your family? What do they look forward to most?

Today a homemaker committed to nesting and mothering is often seen as an inferior person. If she teaches someone else's children, she is given the title of teacher. If she teaches her own children, she's just a mother. If she chooses paint, wallpaper, and fabric for others, she's an interior decorator. If she decorates her own home, she's just a homemaker. While this isn't fair, it is good to know that you are being trained in many professions while being a mother!

I love my roles as a wife and mother and now grandmother—and I continually work to keep our nest warm. When we were raising our kids, I worked at organizing my time to care for them so I had time for other activities at church, the children's school, or at home. Let me encourage you today as an older woman to a younger woman to keep your nest warm. It's what God has called you to do.

Simple Pleasures

- Make a large batch of chocolate chip cookies and invite neighbor children over to enjoy them.
- Deliver a batch of cookies to an elderly person you know from church.
- Take time to visit with this person. Share in fellowship.

Wisdom for Living

Father, how can I create comfort for my children?
What will they remember from today? Please guide my ways
so that I can invest in the most important job of all—motherhood.

237

Money Know-How

Wealth and honor come from you;
you are the ruler of all things. In
your hands are strength and power
to exalt and give strength to all.

1 CHRONICLES 29:12

"You may say to yourself, 'My power and the strength of my hands have produced this wealth for me.' But remember the LORD your God, for it is he who gives you the ability to produce wealth" (Deuteronomy 8:17-18).

Are you living within your means? If so, you are choosing to live a life of more freedom. There might be some tough times for your family, but if you buy into the myth that your family needs more things, then you will never be content.

There's no quick way to get rich, but I can offer you a quick way to get smart about money. Do not be enticed by debt. First, credit cards don't give you a higher standard of living—they'll be your ruin. Second, keep good financial records. They don't have to be fancy, just accurate—and available. Use lists, file boxes, or even decorated shoe boxes for monthly statements. Make lists of your debt and set payoff goals.

If you're married, make sure you are part of the money management know-how in your family. I can't tell you how many women I know who have lost their husbands and then were in the dark about their finances. Be involved so you know what's happening, especially for the financial protection of your children.

And don't forget to have a heart of gratitude. Your means belong to the Lord. Be a good steward of what you are given.

Simple Pleasures

- Cut away the fat in your over-budgeted household.
- Reduce your credit card usage to one well-managed card.
- Cancel the other cards. Don't just stop using them.

Wisdom for Living

I see my home and my family and am grateful
for these blessings. I pray for wisdom and discernment
when it comes to finances. But more than material gain,
my heart longs for spiritual wealth, Lord.

My Recovery Kit

My comfort in my suffering is this:
your promise preserves my life.

PSALM 119:50

Once when I was recovering from surgery, a dear friend shared her creativity with me in a very special way. She showed up in my hospital room with a "recovery kit." In a pretty basket were twelve separately wrapped gifts labeled Day 1, Day 2, Day 3, and so on. There was a sweet card, a refrigerator magnet, a puzzle, a bag of potpourri, a can of chicken soup, a jar of that "bubble stuff" to "blow away my misery." She even put in an apple to keep the doctor away. There were "thank you" stickers and even some candy. It was such fun, and I so enjoyed the friendship she shared with her gift of creativity, which, of course, was really the gift of herself.

This same concept works well for any celebration or hard time a friend or child might be facing. Is your child worried about starting middle school? Create a 12 days of school countdown with small gifts that will excite them about school: a new notebook, gel pens, an item of clothing they wanted, a journal, a certificate good for a pizza they can redeem during their first week of school. Instead of spending days caught up in worry, your child will look forward to each new day's surprise.

Pretty simple, wouldn't you say?

Simple Pleasures

- Create a recovery kit for a friend in need.
- Make a spare and keep it handy for a time when you might need it!
- Wear a brightly colored scarf on a day when you are lacking energy.

Wisdom for Living

Lord, I love to show people they are loved.
The joy I feel in loving others comes from You. Thank You
for the gift of creativity that opens up a world of ways
to express kindness to those You have placed in my life.

239

Build a Clubhouse

The LORD is my strength and my song; he has become my salvation. He is my God, and I will praise him, my father's God, and I will exalt him.

Did you ever build a clubhouse or a fort as a child? Or cover a table with blankets and crawl inside your cozy nest? It reminds me of Psalm 34:7: "The angel of the LORD encamps around those who fear him, and he delivers them." That's what the Lord has done for me. I can feel it! Even in my pain and fear, I can feel the protection of prayers and vigilant love.

So I stand on this promise that no matter what happens, all's well. I believe the Lord will deliver me from my current danger in His time and in His way. In the meantime, He's keeping a close watch to keep me safe. You know what? I continually feel His presence. He is always near.

I hope that by sharing the security I have found in the Lord, you too will seek His comfort for your life. What hurts you today or requires God's healing? Can you give these things over to Him in prayer right now? Your deliverer listens and spreads His arms wide to protect His precious child. Go to Him.

Simple Pleasures

- Bring in large leaves from the yard and create a grand bouquet for your entryway.
- Pile up leaves and take turns with your children jumping over them and in them.
- Laugh a lot today.

Wisdom for Living

Let me trust Your security, Lord.
May I be a woman who stands in awe
of Your mighty power and love. In Your presence
I am safe, warm, and always Your child.

Just a
Few Tricks

May your unfailing love be my comfort, according to your promise to your servant.

PSALM 119:76

How do you receive comfort? Through sights, sounds, textures, tastes, and scents? I love them all! And each can add a special sense of emotional comfort to your home. Try burning a scented candle on a dresser or put soft pillows on the sofa. Sachets in the cupboards and closets can take away musty smells. A wool coverlet draped over the back of the sofa or a footstool close to a chair is very inviting. After your quiet time in the morning, play gentle background music or praise songs to fill your home with God's presence. Music has a wonderful way of entering your heart and encouraging you. Your family and visitors will also feel these comforts.

All of these add that special homelike atmosphere to the place where you live. Even a half-done puzzle, a needlework project in a basket, or a book with a marker can leave one with a feeling of continuity and comfort. Have a daily devotional out on the table so that your family can be filled with God's Word whenever they have a few unplanned moments.

Surround yourself with expressions of God's heart. This is the best way to create a sense of home.

Simple Pleasures

- Sip cider from a mug on your front step.
- Buy yourself some soft mittens to enjoy all season long.
- Purchase an extra pair and give them to a shelter or local Goodwill outlet.

Wisdom for Living

Encouragement. Love. Comfort. Beauty. I will fill my home with these evidences of You, Lord.

Problems? Who, Me?

Consider it pure joy, my brothers, whenever you face trials of many kinds, because you know that the testing of your faith develops perseverance.

JAMES 1:2-3

Problems? I don't think so. I wake up each morning trying to eliminate all the problems I encounter. Too often I think no good can come from having problems! Do you think that too? Well, both of us need to think again.

The Bible says problems strengthen our Christian walk. So be glad—yes, *glad*—that you have problems. Problems do seem to make me more humble—and more appreciative—of what God is trying to do in my life. A world without problems would be a world without solutions. A world without questions would be a world without answers. If you reflect on your faith journey, think just how many times your connection and deeper understanding of God involved a solution to a problem or an answer to a question. Problems help us see God for who He is. Healer, Creator, and omnipotent director of our lives.

Here's my prayer. "God, thanks for loving me. I see what You are attempting to do when You give me problems. But could You start out slowly? I really don't want to become a spiritual giant too quickly! Give me the insights I need to be pleasing to You."

Simple Pleasures

- Right after dinner, store meal-sized portions of leftovers for simple lunches this week.
- Place a vinyl tablecloth on the car floor behind the front seats for easy cleanup after a road trip.
- Create a weekly calendar. Review it each Sunday with the family.

Wisdom for Living

God, You know everything there is to know about the world and about me. Just little me with my problems. And You pay attention to my questions and struggles. Thank You!

Live to the Fullest

Heal me, O LORD, and I will be healed; save me and I will be saved, for you are the one I praise.

JEREMIAH 17:14

Because of illness, I've spent a lot of hours these past few years in doctors' offices. And I've met a lot of people who have received bad news. It's given me a new appreciation for the simple things of life—sleep, walking, running, heartbeats, husband, children, grandchildren. Things I used to take for granted. Now I find myself taking moments several times a day to thank God for my blessings. I don't want to leave out the smallest reason for appreciation.

You know what? This has been a wonderful experience for me. It has made me appreciate what I have. The glass is truly half full and not half empty! Here's a simple tip for you. Make it a daily habit to pause and give thanks to God for your many blessings. If you are going through a bad time right now, I do understand how hard it can be to experience joy in the middle of pain. But it can happen. The two can coexist because God works to mend the spirit.

And when life is good, try to empathize with those who are experiencing a trial. Try to serve them and express your thankfulness for them and who they are. Pray for them and tell God you appreciate all that He does in your life.

Simple Pleasures

- Take a bubble bath in the middle of the day. Enjoy pampering yourself.
- Play your favorite worship CD. Sit down, close your eyes, and spend time with God.
- Take a short nap during your lunch break. It will revive you.

Wisdom for Living

God, I have so many blessings in my life. Once I start listing them, I cannot stop. Help me to experience joy even in times of pain. Help me to appreciate my blessings when all is well.

I'm So Human

O my soul, why be so gloomy and discouraged? Trust in God!

PSALM 43:5 TLB

I become upset when I act so human! I know what I should do, but then something gets in the way. I get in the way.

In the Scripture above, the psalmist is expressing this same idea. Oh, soul, why be discouraged? Why be upset when you have God to trust? Then the psalmist says: "I shall again praise him for his wondrous help; he will make me smile again, for he is my God!" Don't you love that? When my spirit becomes gloomy, I must continually trust in God.

I so appreciate this quote: "Christ does not force our will. He only takes what we give Him." Despite what's happening in our lives, we can say loud and clear: "We will not fear!" I encourage you to use some quiet time today or within the next week to go to God's Word and seek His assurance and comfort. Find a passage to memorize that gives you strength and is a reminder to trust in Him. And the next time you are afraid or too human, you will hear God's words in your heart and mind. They will come to you just as you need them, and they will remind you who is in charge.

Time and time again, God has given me the confidence that I can believe in Him for the future. Of course you are human! And every time that becomes very evident, know that He is your refuge and strength.

Simple Pleasures

- Accept your humanity, but strive to be Christlike in all things.
- Speak your fear out loud to the Lord. Give it to Him today.
- Hire your own children to rake leaves for a neighbor in need of help.

Wisdom for Living

Dear Lord, You are my source of strength. Sometimes I am so discouraged by my own behavior or failings. I give them over to You. Make them into things of beauty. Things that serve You.

The Cozy Areas

May those who love you be secure. May there be peace within your walls.

PSALM 122:6-7

Where in your house does everyone love to gather? I'll bet it's the living room or family room, regardless of the size of your home, apartment, condo, motor home, or even a boat if you live in southern California where we do. The "sitting room" is where family and friends gather. It's the heart of your home. It deserves your most creative efforts to make it both beautiful and cozy. Besides, it's also where everyone will see and appreciate what you've done to make it comfortable.

Add touches to this gathering place that will bless members of your family. Lots of books for your always-reading daughter, a small writing table where you can pen your letters each week, a large comfortable couch where your son can sit and do his homework. Fill the room with colors that are soothing and that express the family's personality as well as your own. Whatever decorating scheme you use, remember that you should always work toward nurturing the spirit as well as comforting the body. When you do that, you'll have a space where all the people you love just love to be!

Simple Pleasures

- Talk about your favorite holiday traditions with your family.
- Have a child read Scripture while the family enjoys the warmth of a fire in the fireplace.
- Set up a game table and start a new family puzzle.

Wisdom for Living

Lord, I long to gather together those I love.
Let me embrace them with Your love and reflections of that love.
May they always feel welcome.

Caring Through Friendship

> Will you rely on him for his great strength? Will you leave your heavy work to him?
>
> JOB 39:11

When you think of true friends, you most likely think of someone who extended help to you in a time of need. Today, think about your own ministry of caring through friendship. Who can you be a friend to at a time when they really need one?

Create postcard greetings for birthdays and anniversaries. Organize a food pantry for needy families or families in crisis. For funerals, provide home-cooked meals. Pack gift boxes with candies and cookies individually wrapped to send to servicemen and women or college students away from home for the first time. Put in boxes of raisins, nuts, and bags of popcorn. And include an encouraging greeting. Create a "wish" list from your missionaries and get people in the church to fulfill the wishes. Provide baby-sitting services for parents who need a break.

Get some of the men in the church to offer a "car fixing" day for single parents, widows, or seniors. Invite one or two single moms over for a weekend. Help them arrange overnight care for their children (maybe your own children are old enough to help with that?), and treat these women to a bed-and-breakfast experience.

There's so much we can do as women to reach out in loving care. We just need to get started. What is holding you back? Extend yourself and extend God's love.

Simple Pleasures

- Make a meal for a single mom who is feeling overwhelmed.
- Be a passive listener to a friend experiencing trials.
- Call a friend who's ill to see if she or her family needs anything from the store.

Wisdom for Living

Open my eyes to the needs of others, Lord.
Let me look for ways to be a friend.

A Little Appreciation

Even in darkness light dawns for the upright, for the gracious and compassionate and righteous man.

PSALM 112:4

Are you looking for just a little appreciation? Maybe a lot? If you are mom to little ones, they either cannot express their thanks or they don't know how to. If your kids are older, their spoken appreciation sometimes is immediately followed by a request for a favor or a material item. Not exactly the heartfelt show of love you desire.

Let's take some time today to appreciate you...a busy mom! With the rush of getting things ready for the holidays, maybe a simple "thank you" wouldn't hurt. What do you think? When I talk with burned-out women, their number one complaint is that no one in the family appreciates them. Seldom do they hear, "That was a great meal." "Thanks for washing and ironing my clothes." "The house always looks so good." The moms I talk to just want someone to notice—to appreciate. Zephaniah 3:17 says: "He will rejoice over you with great gladness" (NLT). He notices your worthy desires and your efforts. He is shouting with joy at all you are doing in His name! Fully immerse yourself in this appreciation from the Lord. It is very real, and it will become your source of strength and inspiration when you need it most.

Simple Pleasures

- List three ways you have helped another person this week.
- List three times that you felt most joyful in your giving of time and effort.
- List three ways God shows you His love and appreciation.

Wisdom for Living

Lord, I come to You feeling tired and unappreciated.
Renew my spirit with Your gracious love. Let me breathe in
Your love and know that as Your child, I am fully, eternally loved.

December

THE SPIRIT OF JOY

Using a Planner

When anxiety was great within me, your consolation brought joy to my soul.

PSALM 94:19

When you flip the calendar from November to December, do you become anxious? Is there a frantic pace to your holiday preparations? Christmas was meant to be enjoyed, and by planning ahead you can give yourself the gifts of time and peace.

Begin right now and schedule your activities week by week. It will lessen the last-minute rush to get everything done. Make the activities surrounding Christmas the kind of expressions that are worthwhile. Set up a "to do" list planner. Use a big shopping list to record all the errands, groceries, and gifts to buy. Your calendar allows you to work the activities into a weekly schedule. Other handy lists are a Christmas card record, a gifts-given record, and a gifts-received record. A shopping guide is the perfect place to note sizes and preferences for everyone. And be sure to have a hospitality chart for any holiday parties you are hosting or attending. These days, a schedule of the children's parties is important to keep alongside your own. Many youth groups and school groups have programs and gatherings that will round out your holiday with family time and a bit of car pooling.

Whew! You're almost ready. Now sit back and have a cup of tea—my treat!

Simple Pleasures

- Will you have family visiting from far away? Plan a group portrait.
- Sift through old Christmas cards and photos. Savor these memories today.
- Place slices of orange in apple cider.

Wisdom for Living

Lord, help me focus on the reason for the season.
Lift my eyes to Your height of glory and not to
the material wants that surround me.

Plan Ahead—
Especially at
Christmas

Come, let us sing for joy to the
Lord; let us shout aloud to the
Rock of our salvation.

Psalm 95:1

I looovvveee Christmas! It's my favorite time of year. I so enjoy having friends and family over—hearing my favorite carols on the radio—and decorating the house in reds and greens from top to bottom! Okay, before you accuse me of being "little Miss Christmas," just know that "keeping it simple" (well, as simple as you can) is what makes it work during the holidays!

If you have ever found yourself wishing you could postpone Christmas instead of relishing this special season, you are in need of a new approach. There are so many activities to look forward to, and all of them occur in a few short weeks. I use a handy game plan to keep up with all the details. By planning ahead when you need to decorate and bake and wrap those last-minute gifts, you can enjoy the season so much more.

The key is to do a little at a time and in priority order. For gifts you need to mail to relatives, start shopping earlier in the year. If you will be attending a few gatherings, select or make simple hostess gifts in advance. If you see something perfect, buy five of them and keep them on hand for those last-minute invitations.

I hope this is your best Christmas ever—one with time to enjoy friends and the real meaning of the season!

Simple Pleasures

- Play Christmas music and begin arranging furniture for holiday gatherings.
- Pray over your home. Let this be a season reflecting God's joy.
- Think of the holiness of the season, not the hecticness.

Wisdom for Living

Pour out on me the spirit of Christmas, Lord.
Never let this season go by in a blur. I want to live in Christmas
fully so that it stays with me throughout the year.

Who Started This Anyway?

On that day they offered great sacrifices, rejoicing because God had given them great joy. The women and children also rejoiced.

NEHEMIAH 12:43

Christmas can be the one time of year when you hear from family and friends who live far away. That is such a wonderful part of this season. Nothing cheers my day like getting a note from an old friend or reading a clever Christmas newsletter. Some people don't like these impersonal forms of communication, but sometimes they are the perfect way to catch up with a busy family's annual happenings.

We collect all of our holiday cards in a big basket and enjoy them the whole season. Did you know it was a procrastinating Englishman named Henry Cole who began the Christmas card tradition? In 1843, Henry was behind in his correspondence and wanted to make everything right with a nice Christmas note to end the year. His idea led to a mass marketing of holiday cards that has grown in ways that would certainly shock old Mr. Cole.

Take time to choose your cards. Even though you buy a dozen or more of the same image and sentiment, cards are your personal expression. They remind our friends of our hope in Jesus Christ and say "I love you" to those we care about. Don't forget to have your children help you with the cards. They can be in charge of addressing them or inserting your family photo into the envelope. Staying in touch is a family affair.

Simple Pleasures

- Create a Christmas card writing basket with pens, stamps, and stickers.
- Take some time to write a few cards early in the season.
- Sip a special holiday blend tea to get the holiday started.

Wisdom for Living

*Father, I know that communication is connection.
Let me rejoice in hearing from old friends. Each one
has been a blessing during a part of my life. Hearing from them
adds to my gratitude for all You have given me.*

Make It Yourself

You will be made rich in every way so that you can be generous on every occasion.

2 CORINTHIANS 9:11

Everyone loves the special touch in a gift of your own creation. Make a batch of bran muffins. You can give the recipe and six fresh-baked muffins in a decorative tin. Wrap clear cellophane around the tin and put a pretty bow on top. I can guarantee you it will be a hit! Or buy a gift certificate from a favorite restaurant and place it in a clear take-out box—an unused one! Add colorful tissue and a ribbon. Simple but fun!

Do your friends have a favorite kind of meal? Fill a basket with all the fixin's for an Italian dinner or a Tex-Mex lunch. Just think, while you are out doing your grocery shopping you could also be picking up the ingredients for these homemade gifts. Now that is a way to conserve your time and energy this holiday season.

Fill a shoe box with small items from the dollar store, cover it with wrapping paper, and give it to a child. Make every gift you give personal and from the heart. It's a season to give from a spirit of overflowing love and gratitude for Jesus Christ—the greatest gift of all.

Simple Pleasures

- Start reading the Gospels out loud as a family each night.
- Walk in the cold morning and warm up with the exercise.
- Plan a short drive out to the country to enjoy the feel of the season.

Wisdom for Living

These gifts I prepare are symbols of Your love, Lord.
I pray that each recipient sees the true giver
behind my heart—Jesus Christ.

Comfy Kitchens

In the houses of the wise are stores of choice food and oil.

PROVERBS 21:20

I can't say enough about kitchens! Do you feel the same? Or do you think I am crazy? Well, just take a look at some ideas for a comfy kitchen *without* a lot of hassle! You might just learn to love your kitchen unconditionally.

Little lamps in your kitchen will do wonders. Or light a candle. Place it on a windowsill and it puts dirty dishes in a "whole new light." Store fruit in a basket or special bowl. Keep your olive oil and wine vinegar in pretty decanters by your stove. Put on soft music and enjoy the glow! If you have the room, why not tuck a comfy rocking chair in the corner? On cold nights especially, a kitchen can be a great place to warm up and take in the scent of freshly baked cookies or just-popped popcorn.

And try to keep your kitchen free of clutter. It will look more spacious, and you'll be a bit more inspired! Take a look at your counters right now. What really needs to be on the surface area? Anything that can be placed in the cupboard for easy retrieval, do it. Too many items, even clean items or appliances, can make the room feel messy. So step into the kitchen like a visitor and take in the first impression.

Love your kitchen by making it a place of hospitality and family time.

Simple Pleasures
* Put up a lot of little white lights inside.
* Drape sheer fabric around lights that frame a window.
* Turn to your prayer journal for moments of solitude today.

Wisdom for Living
O God, thank You that my kitchen is a place to share blessings.
To offer food to the hungry. To give rest and nutrients for energy
to the tired. To say "here you are always welcome" to the least of these.

Toss Me That Basket

He prays to God and finds favor with him, he sees God's face and shouts for joy; he is restored by God to his righteous state.

JOB 33:26

Gather up all those baskets you don't know what to do with! It's a project day for you and me. We're going to make some simple gifts you'll be delighted to give this Christmas.

Baskets filled with fun items make a great gift. Soaps, a shower cap, bubble bath, a washcloth, a candle—and you've got a wonderful basket gift. Or how about a basket for your son-in-law that has car wax, a chamois cloth, Armor-All, and a litter bag for the car? Children are easy. Use games, small toys, books, a teddy bear, dolls, trucks, and puzzles. What fun you can have just putting these together. Get your children to help you shop for items for grandma and grandpa. Let them load up the basket. If you have a bunch to do or decide to create small versions for your children to give to friends, set aside an afternoon for them to watch a favorite holiday video while they create a Christmas basket assembly line. They will have a great time preparing the gifts and will feel a part of the season.

Basket gifts are also great for your neighbors and your children's teacher. Best of all, a basket is easy to deliver. Grab it and go. Everyone will love this creative expression of your friendship.

Simple Pleasures

- Create a holiday-survival basket for yourself. Fill it with tea, chocolate, a new book, all your favorite things. Make one for a friend and deliver it to her as a surprise.
- Play your favorite Christmas music as you wrap gifts.
- Go to the bookstore and find a new Christmas novel.

Wisdom for Living

*Lord, each basket I prepare represents
Your bounty of blessings in life. May each gift given
reflect this abundance of joy we all receive.*

It Doesn't Have to Be Perfect

I do not hide your righteousness in my heart; I speak of your faithfulness and salvation. I do not conceal your love and your truth from the great assembly.

PSALM 40:10

Have you ever not invited someone into your home because it was too messy? You stall outside the door and imagine the marking pens on the kitchen floor, the coloring books on the dining room table, the dishes from breakfast in the sink. So you go against your inclination to extend your hospitality.

When we do this (I have done the same thing), we are forgetting what hospitality really is. It is caring. It is connecting with people. It is not entering our homes in a cleanliness contest.

You know, it doesn't take much—just the heart to care for your guests. When my mother was well into her seventies, she lived in a one-room efficiency apartment. But she extended her hospitality to her guests by offering them a cup of tea or coffee along with some banana bread or cookies. Her visitors always felt special as they sipped tea in real china cups. Mom usually made sure there was also a flower in a drinking glass and a candle on the table. These touches of welcome say "I care!"

Many times we feel things have to be perfect. We want to have the right time, the right house, the right food. But who's to say what's right? All it really takes is the warm, caring attitude of a loving heart.

Simple Pleasures

* Prepare a basket of special food treats for a family that is struggling to make ends meet.
* Tell your children just how much you love them and why.
* Make banana bread and give it to a new neighbor with the recipe.

Wisdom for Living

*Father, turn my focus from personal perfection
to perfect hospitality from the heart.
May I take advantage of every opportunity I have
to open my heart and home to those You send my way.*

Love Thy Neighbor

> *But the angel said to them, "Do not be afraid. I bring you good news of great joy that will be for all the people."*
>
> LUKE 2:10

If there are many people on your Christmas gift list, let me help you out with a few simple ideas that will show your neighbors—especially the elderly—that you care!

Involve your children or grandchildren in a cookie-baking day. It's a wonderful time to grow closer and give them a little experience in the kitchen. Bake and decorate cookies and then put them on colorful paper plates and wrap in clear cellophane wrap. A festive bow is all the cookies need to be a wonderful surprise for neighbors. And delivering them personally with your children is a wonderful chance to visit the elderly and neighbors you don't always see.

Another way to create in the kitchen is to make dough ornaments. Tie ribbons at the top, have the children make homemade cards, and deliver your family's own ornament-of-the-year. This might just turn into a tradition and an easy gift solution for the neighbors and even church friends on your list.

Whew! This is a busy time, isn't it?

Simple Pleasures

- Plan a day to go ice skating with your kids. Even an indoor rink will suit the season.
- Make scarves out of fleece as simple hostess gifts and gifts for your children's friends.
- Write down Scripture verses on parchment paper. Roll them and tie with ribbon. Use these as ornaments and impromptu cards.

Wisdom for Living

Wonderful smells from the kitchen remind me of my childhood.
Oh, how I want to make this season a memorable one
for my children and for those around me. Help me to do this, Lord.

Dated Ornaments Are Fun

> A cheerful look brings joy to the heart.
>
> PROVERBS 15:30

At this time of year, it really is the thought that counts! In fact, people get so caught up in the stress of shopping that when they experience a touch of thoughtfulness, it is refreshment for their spirit.

A fun gift idea is to give a "dated" ornament each year. Take the time to find the perfect ornament for that special someone's interests or personality. Write the year on the back to make it a special keepsake. Some of our trimmings go back 15 to 20 years. It's so special to see when they became part of the tradition at our home. Or when you're visiting friends, you can even slip an ornament on their tree. Just attach a small gift tag. Then when they're taking down the tree, it will be a nice after-Christmas surprise!

When the giver does not make an elaborate show of the actual giving, the gift is more precious to the recipient. So remember, it's the thought that counts. Be creative—there's no end to what can be made into a gift.

Simple Pleasures

- Create a twelve prayers of Christmas for your family.
- Say these together around the dinner table.
- Ask God to bring someone into your life who needs His joy.

Wisdom for Living

Lord, I want loving thoughts of friends to be reflected in my actions and efforts throughout the year. Help me to decorate a friend's season with an ornament of good cheer and happy thoughts this holiday.

Make Celebrating a Tradition

Nehemiah said, "Go and enjoy choice food and sweet drinks, and send some to those who have nothing prepared. This day is sacred to our Lord. Do not grieve, for the joy of the LORD is your strength."

NEHEMIAH 8:10

Let's plan a party! A celebration sure to please everyone that does not involve weeks of planning. These few simple ideas I have for you can help you get started. Once you start the tradition of simple celebrations, you will be hooked. Get ready. Get set. Go.

Mealtimes can be party times. Little touches make a big difference. Try putting your whipped butter in a white pottery crock, add some flowers in a vase, and my favorite…candles, candles, candles! For a festive touch, gift wrap place settings with wide ribbon. Celebrate your cultural heritage and throw a theme party. Play appropriate music, prepare ethnic foods, enjoy who you are. Thank-you notes are a must after you've taken part in a celebration at someone else's home. But you can thank your guests as well. The next time you have company, surprise them by writing a thank-you note as soon as they leave. Thank them for sharing your event and your life.

Express your joy and gratefulness to God for all He's done by creating a tradition of celebrations in your family.

Simple Pleasures

- In your home, create a festive feel and also one of calm and comfort.
- Encourage your children to think of ways to show Jesus this season.
- Fill a basket with packets of cocoa or cider so guests and children can help themselves.

Wisdom for Living

Thank You, Father, for traditions that celebrate who we are and the people we love. They help us reflect Your joy in our lives. Every day is a reason to celebrate!

Tips and Gifts to Make Your Season Bright

Give, and it will be given to you.
A good measure, pressed down,
shaken together and running over,
will be poured into your lap.

LUKE 6:38

Don't you just love a grab bag? Reach in and pull a simple treasure out of this grab bag of holiday ideas that might make your season easier.

Here's a tip my mother taught me: If you cover dried fruits or nuts with flour before adding them to the batter—guess what? They don't sink to the bottom during baking. Play a lot of Christmas music. It's the best mood setter for your holiday party. And when you set the table for that party, add some fun with a gingerbread man propped by each person's water glass with a name tag around his neck.

Children will love this Christmas gift idea! Roll up a dollar bill (or more if the child is older) and put it into a balloon. Mail it along in a card with instructions to blow it up and pop it! For another busy mom, how about making and giving her an actual grab bag of these ideas and more of your own. Just write them down on small pieces of parchment paper, tie each with a satin ribbon, and toss into one of those colorful gift bags you can buy at any card store. Voilà. You have a gift that keeps on giving.

Simple Pleasures

* Spend ten minutes each morning in prayer for your neighbors.
* Watch a favorite classic Christmas movie with your children today.
* Buy a new pair of pajamas for yourself. Think cozy!

Wisdom for Living

Father, what ideas have You given me that might inspire another busy mom? I will watch for ways to not only simplify my holiday, but to help others do the same.

Napkins "Ring" in the Season

From the fullness of his grace we have all received one blessing after another.

JOHN 1:16

Maybe because I love surprises, I cannot resist adding holiday cheer to unexpected places. My favorite additions to a table setting are napkin rings. They set off a pretty centerpiece and tie all your colors together. If you don't have a set of them, or if you are expecting a crowd larger than your napkin ring collection, a new set can be made in minutes. Cover empty toilet paper rolls with lace and cut the rolls two or three inches in width. If you have the time, you can add more detail like ribbons and beads. Even silver bells!

I've also used napkin rings to hold special wishes for guests. Take a paper towel tube and cut it in two-inch widths. Cut each ring so it opens. Write a Scripture or blessing inside. Then with your glue gun, cover the outside with ribbon and leave the tails long enough to tie a bow. Slide your napkin through the ring. When it's untied, there's the message just for that person.

When you take extra steps to decorate your home for the holiday, you send a message of comfort and warmth to everyone who sits at your table, exchanges season's greetings, and joins your family to celebrate the birth of the Savior.

Simple Pleasures
* Keep your decorations simple and cozy.
* Find out if there are sleigh rides anywhere near you. Arrange for a family outing.
* Give any anxieties you have over to the Lord.

Wisdom for Living
I can't imagine Mary's surprise when the angel visited her.
Father, thank You for the opportunity to make
every Christmas a celebration of the surprise
that gave the world its greatest gift.

Sharing Is Caring

He chose to give us birth through the word of truth, that we might be a kind of firstfruits of all he created.

JAMES 1:18

You probably know me well enough to know I love to talk about decorating, making more hours in your day, providing a loving, welcoming home, and tea parties! But in the end, what really matters is the sharing.

You want your house beautiful, comfortable, and cozy. But whatever you do to walls and windows—or kitchens and bathrooms—don't forget your most wonderful adornment! It's your spirit of hospitality, your willingness to share your home and your life in Christ with others. Don't wait until everything's perfect. Something will always need fixing or painting. Love what you have and invite others to share the bounty. Your gracious welcome will fill in the gaps.

Do you have new neighbors? Invite them over for cookies. Did a family just join your church? Call them to introduce yourself. Do you have an elderly friend? Have them over for dinner to be a part of your young family.

Your home will always be the most beautiful when you stretch out your arms in welcome!

Simple Pleasures

The ache for home lies in all of us;
the place where we can go as we are and not be questioned.
—MAYA ANGELOU

Wisdom for Living

Come in, Lord. This is Your home.
Let me prepare it for You and for those You send to me.

*Flesh gives birth to flesh, but the
Spirit gives birth to spirit.*

JOHN 3:6

Consider decorating your child's room if you haven't done that yet. Start with some simple ideas that will not disrupt the use of the room at any time. If you can take a weekend to paint and really roll up your sleeves, I have some ideas to get you and your child headed in a creative direction.

Circus themes are popular and fun. You can paint walls and the ceiling to resemble the inside of a circus tent. Use clown stripes for curtains. Or pick a nautical theme with ocean blue carpet and anchors and life preservers for decoration. Paint a tree trunk in a corner of the room for a wonderful fantasy of living in a tree house. You could even hang a little wooden swing from the ceiling for a doll or stuffed animal. We always kept plenty of storybooks to read and look at in our children's rooms.

Host family story times in a child's room or trade off so that you visit each child's room once a week. Go a step further and be the story lady in the neighborhood. Plan to host neighbor kids for cookies, punch, and a short story time on Saturday mornings for 30 minutes to one hour. It just might get a few kids to pull away from Saturday morning cartoons and all those commercials once in awhile!

If you want to start simply, go with a holiday theme to help your child celebrate.

Simple Pleasures

- Read a favorite childhood story to yourself and your children.
- Write some ideas for a children's story. You never know what you can do!
- Encourage your children to think of stories. They can role-play using toys and decorating themes in their bedroom.

Wisdom for Living

*Life is about living! Dear Lord, let me live fully
each day and find time for laughter so that Your joy
is always evident in my home.*

Family Together Times

She will give birth to a son, and you are to give him the name Jesus, because he will save his people from their sins.

MATTHEW 1:21

It didn't take us long as a family to realize we needed a set time to be together. Times to discuss important topics. Family conferences and fun *can* be combined! In fact, we had some of our best discussions assembling puzzles together. This takes pressure off children for direct communication. It is amazing what they share under the security of another activity. If you take a child to one of those pottery painting shops, you will see what I mean. View family movies or videos and have everyone share a favorite memory. Plan a fix-it night so everyone has a project to work on or maybe the same project. Take before and after photos for motivation. When you are finished, celebrate with apple cider and sugar cookies.

Cooking and baking are ideal "talk" times. So are playing board games, going on picnics, riding bicycles, and working out at the gym. Use holiday times to make and do things together. You know, we're only limited by our imagination. Our family times played a valuable part in building respect and pride in our family. If you haven't done together times in awhile, it might be a bit awkward getting started again, but do it anyway. I guarantee you, they're worth it!

Simple Pleasures

- Plan a together time for you and your husband soon.
- Sing a favorite hymn out loud while you are doing housework. It lifts the spirit!
- Buy a sketchbook and draw pictures of your home, your children, your life. No one has to see these unless you decide to share!

Wisdom for Living

Family time gives us a chance to grow in You, Lord. Bless our time together. Help us grow stronger and kinder toward one another.

A Christmas Tea

You have made known to me the path of life; you will fill me with joy in your presence, with eternal pleasures at your right hand.

PSALM 16:11

You're invited to begin the Christmas season with a very special tea party!

Start off the holiday with a heart full of welcome! I love this time of year. It's a season when we celebrate the birth of our Savior. And it's time for being with friends and family and—you know me—that means a tea party!

Invite a few close friends, a study group, or your sisters, and offer them a time of renewal that will inspire their season. A tea party is perfect for the occasion. Keep it simple, make it beautiful, and celebrate God's gift to you and your friends. It will kick off the holidays on a proper note and prepare your heart and your home for the days of joy to come. Just think, if a few of your friends each hosted a mid-week tea during the month of December, you would have that time of fellowship amid the busyness of your holiday preparations. Now that would evoke the spirit of the season!

By the way, did you know that tea helps relieve fatigue, lift the spirits, and stimulate the mind? Just thought I'd let you know!

Simple Pleasures

- Do you feel the joy yet? Calm your spirit with a CD of praise songs.
- Celebrate the holiday with friends. Don't forget to spend time with these special women.
- Invite your mother to spend a day with your friends.

Wisdom for Living

Lord, infuse my friendships with the warmth of Your love.
May I savor every occasion I have to be among friends.

Where Does the Time Go?

He will be a joy and delight to you, and many will rejoice because of his birth.

LUKE 1:14

Oops—have you waited until the last minute to do your shopping? Well, all is not lost! I would like to offer up some ways to eliminate a bit of that last-minute stress. I don't want you feeling rushed this Christmas. So let's find a way to make your life easier.

Take advantage of wrapping services at your department stores or boutiques. At the time, it can feel like a delay on your busy, last-minute shopping tour. But just think how good it will feel when you get home with ready-to-give presents! That can be a lifesaver.

For those hard-to-please people you keep putting off buying for, how about a gift certificate to a restaurant, an ice-cream shop, or a favorite fast-food place? There's always theater tickets, sports tickets, or annual passes to amusement parks.

Don't forget to use the phone and the Internet! Have a florist make up special arrangements and have them delivered. One of my favorites is a beautiful poinsettia plant. It's always a great gift. Also, use the one-stop method! Give several people on your list the same thing—have a gourmet shop make baskets for you. Or place an Internet order for a special Christmas devotional to be sent to your relatives who live several states away.

Simple Pleasures

- Consider buying presents online for friends who live far away.
- Buy several gift certificates to an area grocery store to give to a family in need.
- Write a Christmas poem to give as a gift to neighbors. Deliver it with a plate of cookies.

Wisdom for Living

*Time is precious, Lord. Help me to use my time wisely.
I long to spend time with You during this season.
Let's meet each morning before I begin my day.*

Thinking of Others

Praise be to the God and Father of our Lord Jesus Christ! In his great mercy he has given us new birth into a living hope through the resurrection of Jesus Christ.

1 PETER 1:3

I love the feeling of spreading the special sounds of the season to friends and neighbors. And caroling is one of the best ways to share the meaning of Christmas with others. Make it a fun occasion of singing and praising God in the songs you select. Include a rest home or a shut-in for your caroling. It's a great way to spread joy to those who may not be able to celebrate with family and friends.

Think of the many people who have lost someone since last Christmas. Maybe even you are struggling with such a loss as the holiday approaches. If so, I pray that God's love and the kindness of family and friends will fill that void with tenderness. I pray that there will be peace instead of cutting pain. If you know someone who faces a difficult holiday, go the extra mile for them. Invite them to a dinner gathering. Offer to take them to your church's candlelight service if it has one. Ask them over for coffee or tea and plan to spend several hours just talking. Christmas is a lonely time of year for some people. Your extra attention will strengthen their broken hearts.

Reach out to those around you and share the love and hope that's only found in our loving Savior.

Simple Pleasures

- Get up a little earlier and turn on those little lights. Enjoy the moment.
- Pray to God and give Him your heart this season.
- Spend more time than money on your Christmas preparations.

Wisdom for Living

God, You know those who need extra care and attention right now.
And You see the places where my own heart is broken.
I pray to be attentive to those in need.
And I pray for Your healing in my own life.

The Empty Chair

*Surely you have granted him
eternal blessings and made him
glad with the joy of your presence.*

PSALM 21:6

Did you know that in Poland an empty chair at the Christmas meal means that Jesus is "welcome at your table"? It's a wonderful way to honor Him. Or use the custom to remember loved ones who can't be with you. The empty chair says they are remembered even though they can't be there. What a powerful, symbolic gesture.

Think of your own family traditions. Do they share the miracle and wonder of the Christ child? Try to bring the awe of a loving Savior to your Christmas celebration. Gather everyone up and attend a special church service this Christmas Day. Or build a roaring fire and read the Christmas story from the Bible. Instead of going to bed on time, bundle up in warm clothes and sit in the yard. Look at the stars and talk about the Star of Bethlehem. As the children get older, have them take turns sharing, in their own way, the events that led to Christ's birth.

Christmas is a sacred time to celebrate family, a warm home, and the joy of being a child of God.

Simple Pleasures

- Reflect on the Christmas story during your devotion time.
- Pray with your husband over each child while he or she is sleeping.
- Walk to a local coffee shop this morning to start your day off.

Wisdom for Living

*Dear God, am I passing on the full joy of Your Son's birth?
All year I look forward to drawing my family together, to pray over
them and with them, and to share the miracle of Christ. Thank You
for the tradition of love You began more than 2000 years ago.*

Shopping Smart

For the LORD your God will bless you in all your harvest and in all the work of your hands, and your joy will be complete.

DEUTERONOMY 16:15

When it comes to Christmas shopping, keep it simple and keep it smart! Write down all the stores you need to go to so as to make as few trips as possible. Take advantage of wrapping services, gift boxes, ribbon, and tissue. Do two things at once. (That won't be anything new!) If you buy something the store is gift wrapping, do other shopping while you're waiting. Use the florist to send unique silk arrangements. They'll often do gift baskets as well.

Involve your children in the true spirit of the Christmas season. "Adopt" another family for the season and have your children choose gifts and make cards for the children in the other family. Children need to feel the joy of giving at Christmas, not just receiving.

Did I already say keep it simple? And by all means, hang on to your sense of humor. Make it fun. Meet up with girlfriends to shop. Plan to go to a matinee once all of your shopping is done as an incentive. While you're at it, plan a coffee, tea, or lunch break. Treat yourself along the way and enjoy the holidays!

Simple Pleasures

- Simple. Simple. Simple. Keep it simple.
- Give your children precious time and energy instead of too many gifts this year.
- For your little ones, involve them in every way you can. Create holiday memories for them that will last a lifetime.

Wisdom for Living

Lord, keep my mind and heart sane and focused on the gift of Your Son during this season. Your generosity and sacrifice inspire me to mirror Your love.

269

Holiday Centerpieces

You make me glad by your deeds,
O LORD; I sing for joy at the
works of your hands.

PSALM 92:4

Reflect the heart of the season in your Christmas decorating style. A holiday centerpiece is the perfect way to have a focal point that will inspire seasonal cheer.

And the best part is you can make them out of whatever you have! I've made arrangements with dried flowers, candles, teacups, ornaments, and even a nativity scene. They can highlight a theme of a party or even the food you're serving. Candy canes are wonderful to use. A group of candles of different heights makes a beautiful table accent. Tie a plaid Christmas bow around the base of your candles.

A wreath set on a glass plate with candles is also very pretty. A wreath is wonderful because you can change the accent pieces depending on the mood of the meal gathering. Dress it up with some poinsettias, pine cones, ribbons, ivy, or holly. Or dress it down with candy canes, colorful packages, and tiny stockings.

Create a centerpiece above the table by hanging Christmas cards from clear nylon thread. It becomes an inexpensive, beautiful mobile. Use your imagination and flair for the festive!

Simple Pleasures

* Make some eggnog for the night your family decorates the tree.
* Turn up the old-time Christmas music and dance with your husband.
* Take turns dancing with your children. Immerse yourself in the spirit of joy.

Wisdom for Living

My faith is the centerpiece of my life. I desire to put You
at the center of all I do throughout the season, Lord.

Other Harvest House Books
by Bob & Emilie Barnes

🍂 🍂 🍂

Books by
Bob & Emilie Barnes

*Minute Meditations™
for Couples*

*A Little Book of Manners
for Boys*

Abundance of the Heart

*15 Minute Devotions
for Couples*

Books by Emilie Barnes

The 15-Minute Organizer

15 Minutes Alone with God

*15 Minutes of Peace
with God*

101 Ways to Lift Your Spirits

*The Busy Woman's Guide
to Healthy Eating*

A Tea to Comfort Your Soul

A Cup of God's Love

A Cup of Hope

A Different Kind of Miracle

*Emilie's Creative
Home Organizer*

*Everything I Know
I Learned from My Garden*

Fill My Cup, Lord

Friends Are a Blessing

Friends of the Heart

Help Me Trust You, Lord

If Teacups Could Talk

An Invitation to Tea

Join Me for Tea

*Keep It Simple
for Busy Women*

Let's Have a Tea Party!

A Little Book of Manners

*Minute Meditations™
for Busy Moms*

*Minute Meditations™
for Women*

More Hours in My Day

The Promise of Hope

Safe in the Father's Hands

*Strength for Today,
Bright Hope for Tomorrow*

Survival for Busy Women

*The Twelve Teas™ of
Christmas*

*The Twelve Teas™
of Friendship*

Books by Bob Barnes

*15 Minutes Alone with God
for Men*

Minute Meditations™ for Men

*What Makes a Man
Feel Loved*